At the Drop of The Flag

Teesside's
Glorious Years Of Motor Sport

1900-1960

By
ERNIE CRUST

Published by
IOTA PUBLISHING

First published 2005
Published by
IOTA Publishing
9a Gypsy Lane
Nunthorpe
Middlesbrough TS7 0DY

E. J. Crust 2005 © text

All rights reserved. No part of this publication may be reproduced, stored in a retrievable system, or transmitted in any form or by any means, electronic, mechanical, photocopying, recording or otherwise, without the prior permission of the publishers and copyright holders.

ISBN 0-9551284-0-4

Also by Iota Publishing:
E .J. Crust 2000. "A Dash Between the Tides:
A Photographic Record of Sand Racing at Saltburn and Redcar 1905 – 1965".

Printed by Thurston Printers
6 Amber Street, Saltburn-by-the-Sea, Cleveland TS12 1DT
Telephone (01287) 623756.
www.thurstonprinters.co.uk

Main Front Cover: Two Pioneer Speedway Riders from Middlesbrough (see page 101)

Back Cover:
This photograph is something of a puzzle as I have been unable to find any evidence of it ever being raced a Saltburn in the 1930s. The small boy in the car is a future Norton and B.S.A. works trials star rider, Rex Young, who thought it was a Dixon Riley. It is more likely to be there as a publicity car from Dixon's Garage on Linthorpe Road, Middlesbrough.
Courtesy of Rex Young

ACKNOWLEDGEMENTS

No book of this type and such diversity of motor sport history can be compiled without the help of numerous people and various official departments, as well as private collections. Despite my best endeavours it was manifestly impossible to trace title to the earlier photographs. If any copyright has been infringed, apologies are due.

I should like to offer special thanks to the following, not in alphabetical or preferential order:
MIKE SMAILES, ADRIAN MCTIERNAN, JIM WRIGHT, MICHAEL WORTHINGTON - WILLIAMS, MIDDLESBROUGH AND DISTRICT MOTOR CLUB, JOHN OGDON, BILL HUTTON (WILF BARKER COLLECTION), MORTON'S MOTORCYCLE MEDIA, DARLINGTON REFERENCE LIBRARY, REX YOUNG, REX RICHARDSON, TONY BANCROFT, HARTLEPOOL HISTORY COLLECTION, JOHN FALCONER, ALAN ENSOLL, RORY SINCLAIR, JIMMY BLOOMER, JEFF CLEWS, ERNIE FOWLER, JOHN WHITFIELD, JULIAN MAJZUB, JOHN COVERDALE, PETER WOLF, GRANT SELLARS, THE AUTOMOBILE, PETER HODGSON, VINTAGE MOTORCYCLE CLUB, THE LATE MR HORACE READING, PETER LLOYD, JOHN SMITH, JACK MOSS – (FOR PHOTOGRAPHS FROM THE THIRSK MOTOR CLUB).

TED WALKER – (FERRET PHOTOGRAPHICS), THE NATIONAL MOTOR MUSEUM (BEAULIEU), EVENING GAZETTE MIDDLESBROUGH - NEWS QUEST NORTHEAST LTD, THE LATE MR. ALF KIRBY, AND THE LATE MR. BILL ZEALAND, ACKRILL NEWSPAPERS LTD., THE EVENING PRESS - YORK (FORMERLY YORKSHIRE GAZETTE), MR. L. BRUCE MIDDLESBROUGH REFERENCE LIBRARY), MR. WILCOX, THE LATE MR. REG PRICE, THE VAUXHALL HERITAGE CENTRE, TONY LYNN, ROBIN COOK, BILL PAGE, IAN DENNY, WALLACE HOLMES, RUSS ARMSTRONG, PHIL PHILO, (editing this and previous "A Dash Between the Tides"), CRAIG PORRITT, THE STOCKTON MUSEUM, MAURICE JENNINGS, RICHARD PILGRIM, THE JACK THREADGALL FAMILY. MIDDLESBROUGH'S DORMAN MUSEUM, TERRY WRIGHT & BOB LIGHT.

I would like to apologise in advance, should any of my research work subsequently prove to be erroneous

Hartlepool Motor Club

Redcar & District
Motor Club

Stockton Motor Club

Middlesbrough & District
Motor Club

The Primrose League

North Eastern Automobile
Association

Darlington & District
Motor Club

PROLOGUE

It is a recognised fact that motor sport was invented by the French when the first automobile race in history was staged between Paris and Rouen on 22nd June 1894, a distance of 78 miles. On 28th November 1895 the American motor manufacturers staged their first race meeting. Unfortunately here in England our motor industry was held back by successive Government restrictions in the Road Traffic Act. It wasn't until the Emancipation Act of 1896 that the speed limit was raised from 4 mph to 12 mph. (This was raised to 20 mph in 1903). It is interesting to note that in 1906 Saltburn Council applied to the North Riding County Council for the imposition of an 8 mph speed limit as motorists were spoiling Saltburn for pedestrian tourists.

Bearing in mind that almost all other forms of transport were horse drawn, the car and motorcycle would be the last thing in the World a horse would have wished to meet! Three years earlier on Whit Monday, when Saltburn's Marine Parade was packed, a horse had been frightened by a car. It bolted, overturning its trap at the foot of Amber Street. Three of the trap's four passengers were injured, a Miss Hodge breaking her collarbone. The request for an 8 mph speed limit was denied! With such incidents it is thought that rising public concern about the plight of horses, particularly in the towns and big cities, was a major factor in slow progress getting public support for the motor transport.

To Middlesbro' Motorists.

Sixteen motor cars and twelve motor cycles have been registered in Middlesbrough as required by the new Act. For the former 26 drivers' licenses have been issued, whilst eight persons are entitled to assume control of motor cycles. The centre of the borough has been fixed as the four corners of the Municipal Buildings, and it is required that all cars within a mile of this shall not exceed ten miles per hour. The limit for cars coming within half a mile of the centre has been fixed for eight miles an hour, whilst within a quarter of a mile drivers will not be allowed to exceed six miles an hour. The half-mile limit covers the busiest parts, and the mile practically the whole municipal borough.

AUTHOR'S NOTE

In compiling this book I have tried to select photographs of a diverse interest that capture some of the most memorable moments in Teesside's long history of motor sport. This random selection is in no way to be accepted as a definitive history as I'm sure it would take many more volumes to achieve this.

I have commenced with some reference to the area's contribution to motor manufacturing which deserves mention and recording for history's sake. Unless of special historical interest, I have restricted the story to clubs' activities in and around Teesside, i.e. MIDDLESBROUGH, STOCKTON, DARLINGTON, HARTLEPOOL, REDCAR, THIRSK, NORTHALLERTON, AND I.C.I. WILTON, THE PRIMROSE LEAGUE AND NORTHEASTERN AUTOMOBILE ASSOCIATION. Of course, apart from these clubs' organised events, I do acknowledge the contribution of the other local clubs in motor sport who annually staged full programmes of excellent sport, notably YORKSHIRE SPORTS CAR CLUB, PICKERING and SCARBOROUGH. We must not forget the efforts of the smaller clubs more associated with social and touring activities, WILTON I.C.I., DORMAN LONG, HEAD WRIGHTSON, BILLINGHAM SYNTHONIA, SOUTH BANK, and I am sure there were more now no longer operating.

The reader will no doubt notice that I have more photographs and reports on some Teesside club events and little on others. I can only say that this was probably due to no local press photographer being in attendance at the event and the club secretary not sending in a report. I only use the best professional quality photographs where available or a good amateur example.

"Yesterday is the playground of all men's hearts"

THE FOUNDATION STONES

In the early years of the 20th century fledgling motor clubs, from the mouth of the River Tees at the North and South Gares along the banks and surrounding countryside for miles up to its source in Upper Teesdale, laid the foundation stones to enable motor sport to flourish. To set the scene, you should imagine a certain way of life many years ago, completely removed from the way we live today. Snobbery was rife. Class differences were rigid, when even the most modest middle-class family would have one domestic servant. Distant travel was mostly for the better off. It was an era when we were fiercely proud of our Country and Empire and were famous for our engineering.

The owner of any type of motor vehicle would need to be someone of means. The average man could perhaps earn between £1 and £2 per week, depending on his skills. It goes without saying that the first owners in the Tees Valley were quite wealthy or upper and middle-class businessmen who were prepared to spend some disposable income on motorised transport. Most of these adventurous young pioneers had little knowledge of the internal combustion engine and its workings. To them it was a status symbol and an emblem of liberation. It wasn't long before small groups of these enthusiasts started meeting up at various field sporting events. At first the motor car owners tend to form clubs for car owners only and likewise the motor cyclist. It was some years before clubs amalgamated while others remained independent.

Historical records are conflicting and riddled with inconsistencies and it is debatable to which town can go the honour of the first organised club in the Teesside area! Broadly speaking the years from 1900-1905 were the years that the Stockton and District Auto, Darlington and Hartlepool and Middlesbrough clubs were established. At this stage in motoring history it was still uncertain as to whether the petrol engine was the best possible source of motive power. In fact the steam motorcar, popular in the USA, was in some circles considered a serious contender, along with the electric car.

It was in 1901 that wealthy Northallerton business man, Mr Ernest Hutton built a rear mounted De Dion engined car of 5 or 6 horsepower with 2-speed belt drive. By 1908 he liquidated his car business and moved to the Napier Works in London and his interests were absorbed into the Napier-built 12-20 horsepower car. Hutton returned to Teesside in the same year to drive a Napier-engined Hutton to victory in three events in the Saltburn Speed Trials.

Arguably the first car on Teesside was a one-and-a-half horsepower Benz in 1896, owned by 21 year-old steel works manager, George Scoby Smith. By the time vehicle registration became compulsory in 1903, he had changed the Benz for a Locomobile which was registered in Middlesbrough as DC1.

Saltburn's Arthur Critchley was a man of vision. He was confident that the internal combustion was the way to go. By 1905 he had designed and built his Chriton 12hp prototype at his Diamond St. garage. The car had an advanced specification for its time. Unfortunately little is known of its performance and only two were built. Arthur Critchley himself can go down in motor sport history as the man who helped to orchestrate the first Saltburn Speed Trials, organized by the Yorkshire Automobile Club in 1906.

On the other side of the Tees, Robert Robinson established his cycle shop in Avenue Road, Hartlepool in 1883, and became the owner of a Benz 3hp car in 1897. Robinsons later became the town's main motorcycle dealer.

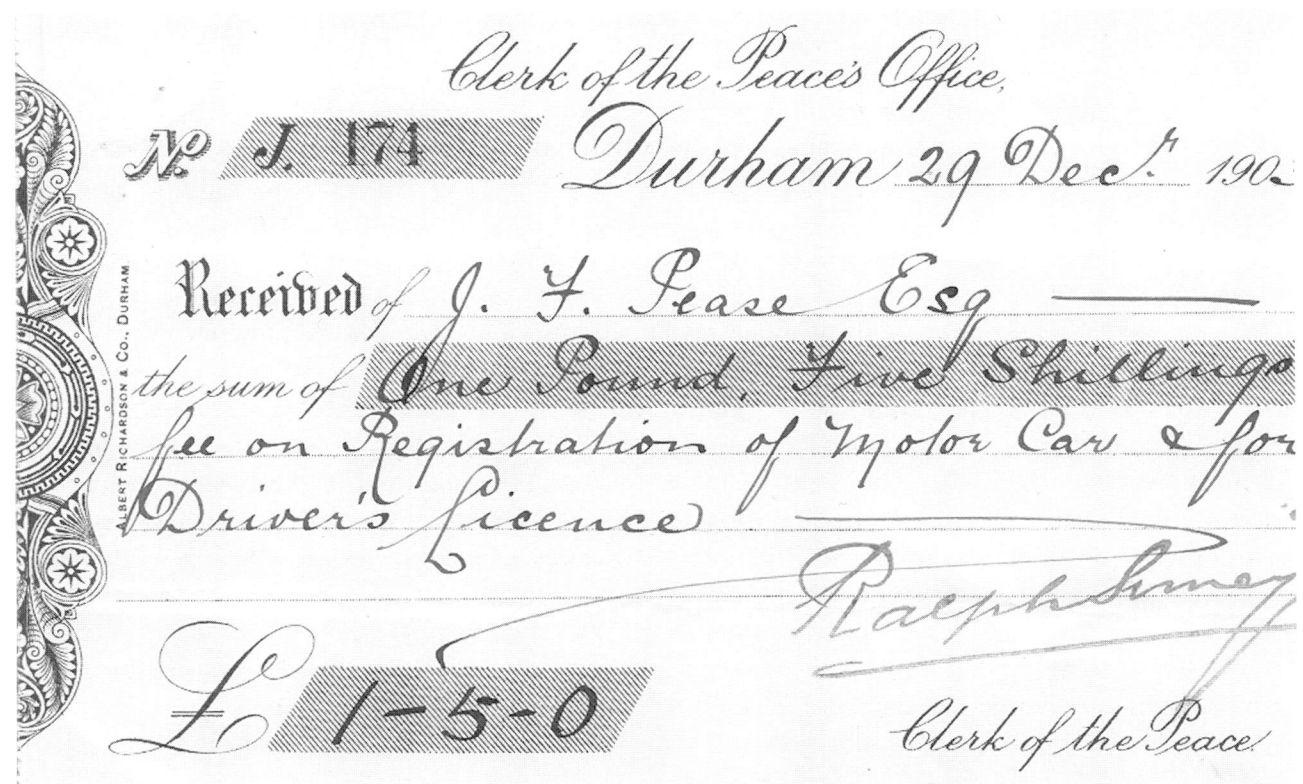

Early driving license issued to John Francis Pease of Darlington which included car registration.
Courtesy of Wallace Holmes

Further rare documents of J.F. Pease, car registration No. J26. Also his membership subscription of the Automobile Club of Great Britain and Ireland 1902
Courtesy of Wallace Holmes

Ordinary Member (Country).   No. 223

THE AUTOMOBILE CLUB OF GREAT BRITAIN AND IRELAND,
— WITH WHICH IS INCORPORATED —
THE SELF-PROPELLED TRAFFIC ASSOCIATION.

Received this .... day of .... August .... 190 2.
of J. Francis Pease Esq., of Darlington
the Sum of Nine Guineas, viz.: Five Guineas being the Ordinary Member's Subscription to the above Club for the year ending 31st December, 190 2, and Four Guineas being Entrance Fee.

Subscription	£5 5 0
Entrance Fee	4 4 0
	£9 9 0

C. Johnson, Secretary.

This delightful picture of an infant member of the Pease family from Darlington proudly and effectively displays one of the family cars - in this instance believed to be a 1903 Voiture le Legere Minerva Type A., probably one of the first cars in Darlington.
Courtesy of Wallace Holmes

Founder of the Middlesbrough & District Motor Cycle Club (1905) Geoff Liddle and his family with their F.N. sidecar outfit at the Richmond meet, 1907.

Mr. Sanderson of 105 Linthorpe Road, Middlesbrough, the first treasurer of Middlesbrough & District Motor Cycle Club, proudly shows off his 1903 2hp Quadrant. Mr. Sanderson was in the outdoor clothing trade and gave talks on the latest motoring clothing available in those pioneering days.

DARLINGTON & DISTRICT AUTOMOBILE ASSOCIATION

Resolutions passed at a meeting held at 1 Victoria Road, Darlington 9th January 1904. J.H. Pease Esq. Woodside, Darlington Presided, and the following gentlemen were also present:-

C.F.Dixon Esq, Raventhorpe, Darlington.
J.P.Pease Esq, Pierremont, Darlington
W. Dudley Richardson Esq, Holmwood, Darlington
J. Edward Hodgkin Esq, Shelleys, Darlington.
E.C. Cox-Walker Esq, Tees View, Croft
G.P. Mounsey Esq, Blackwell Hill, Darlington.
H.W. Sewell, Esq. Fylands, Bishop Auckland
H.S.Streatfeild Esq

Badge of the Automobile Club of Great Britain & Ireland

Mr. Streatfeild having explained the necessity for a local Association to watch the action of local authorities in regard To any proposals for closing road, or imposing the 10 mile limit, It was resolved:-

1. That an Assocation be formed to be called "The Darlington & District Automobile Association",
2. That the objects of the Association shall be:-
    (a) To watch the interests of Motorists generally In this district,.

    (b) To take any steps necessary to prevent any unduly Restrictive action being taken by local Authorities.

Courtesy of the Vintage Motorcycle Club.

In the closing years of the 19th century Teessiders were to see local steel director George Scoby Smith driving his one-and-a-half horsepower Benz. By the time vehicle registration was introduced in 1903 he had changed the Benz for a Localmobile, the first car registered in Middlesbrough as DC1. Evidently he was quite a motor sports supporter as in 1906 at the first Saltburn Speed Trials, driving as 16 power Humber, he won the Sir Hugh Bell Cup. Note that there are no brakes on the Benz other than the wooden block type, which can be seen on the back wheel and operated by the lever on Scoby Smith's left. The coachwork and type of brakes were normal on horse drawn carriages.
Courtesy of Middlesbrough Reference Library

This Tricar Special, built by Mr. Wilcox from Teesside in the 1903-05 period, seems to consist of parts from Singer and B.A.T. The background is thought to be an allotment in South Bank, Middlesbrough close to the River Tees which, it is assumed, was also used by Mr Wilcox as a workshop.
Courtesy of Mr. Wilcox

This home-made special could have De Dion Bouton origins and is thought to be the first car in Cleveland from about 1901-03.
Courtesy of The Dorman Museum, Middlesbrough

West Hartlepool pioneer motorist Dr Albert Edward Morrison was in partnership with Dr Cowley as surgeons in premises on Brougham Terrace. The car is a 1904 De Dion Bouton finished in white with red lining. It was normal practice for a gentleman of this standing to employ a chauffeur.
Courtesy of Hartlepool History Collection

A confident member of the Price family poses for the photographer on the Middlesbrough-made "Cleveland", manufactured prior to the Kaiser war (1914-1918)
Courtesy of Reg Price.

PIONEER MAKERS

THE BOLSOVER STEAM CAR 1902-1919

Bolsover Brothers Ltd of Highfield, Eaglescliffe, and Yarm-on-Tees near the Wesleyan Chapel, were boilermakers and started manufacture of flash-rapid steaming boilers for cars and launches. Harold, born 1879, was a practical man and a trained naval architect. He and his brother, Rowley, who was born 1876 and had fallen from his pony, crippling his leg which had had to be amputated, were firm believers in the use of small steam car engines for cars. After many years of research, tests proved that the system was capable of everything a petrol engine would do. The car's general appearance was not unlike any other car of that era. The most notable difference to a petrol-driven car was the performance. "Bolsover" had a quite rapid turn of acceleration from a standing start and yet was almost silent, with a wisp of steam from the exhaust.

So strong was the belief in the future of the steam car that the brothers published a monthly magazine "Steam Car Development and Steam Aviation". This had a large circulation among steam enthusiasts all over the world and was published until at least 1940. It is difficult to say how many cars were made. Luckily, out of a possible 12 made, one does survive and is undergoing restoration after being shipped back from South Africa where, it is believed, possibly one other car was exported. Car manufacture ceased approximately the period of World War One but a kit of engine castings was available for steam enthusiasts to build up and install in a donor car. One or two exist installed in Austin Seven cars. The Bolsover family moved to Nestling House, Sleights, in the 1930s, continuing business in Whitby, manufacturing their engines until 1950.

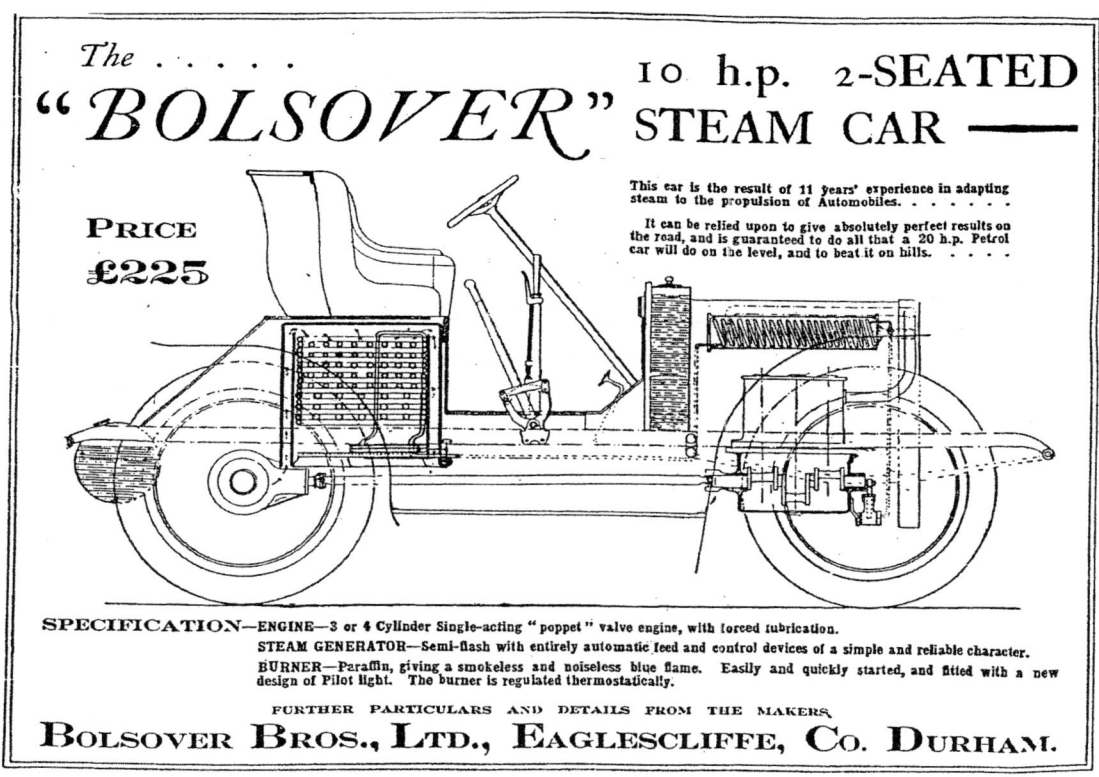

Advertisement for the "Bolsover" 10hp. 2-Seater Steam Car
Courtesy of the Bolsover Family

Drawing of the "Bolsover"
Courtesy of the Bolsover Family

Don't laugh at the idea of steam powered flight! It does work, although not made by Bolsover Brothers. A successful demonstration flight by steam power took place in California in June 1934. It is interesting to note that in 1907, at a Yorkshire Auto Club Hill climb staged at Birkbrow, a Stanley steam car set the fastest time of the day.

THE SHEW

The Seaham Harbour Engine Works (SHEW) was owned by wealthy mines owner The Marquis of Londonderry, who lived on his Wynyard Park estate on the north side of the Tees.

The Works Manager, Mr Allison, had a car, which was said to be of rather ugly appearance, constructed at the Seaham Harbour Works in 1906. It was powered by a vertical twin cylinder, water-cooled Forman Engine made in Coventry. This is the sole example, as it never went into mass-production, and was just used as a hack around the Seaham Harbour Works. The car was abandoned in 1912 in outbuildings on the Wynyard Park and was eventually discovered in 1957 by George Kendrew of Norton, who restored it to its former glory. It was put back on the road and competed in one London to Brighton run. After this it disappeared for a number of years and in recent times came up at auction. Fittingly it now resides at Beamish Museum, County Durham, not that far from it's original birthplace.

During restoration of the Shrew car by George Kendrew it is thought that George constructed a new body which was painted yellow with black stripes. The photograph was taken at a vintage rally in the North of England, George at the wheel!
Courtesy of Bill Zealand

THE CHRITON

Thought to be the only photographs of the sole Chritons ever built by the Critchley Motor Engineering Company, including the prototype with Arthur Critchley at the wheel. The 12hp four seater version, which would have been the basis for the production model, outside the Brownless Coach Builders shop in Diamond Street, Saltburn.
Courtesy of Norman Bainbridge

WADDINGTON & HALL

Piano Makers and Motor Manufacturers
30 Newport Road and Greta St., Middlesbrough

One could not imagine a more diverse business, although the motoring side of the business was adjunct to their main interest. On sifting through the sparse information available on the firm I find conflicting reports in the motoring journals of the 1903-04 period. According to one source the cars were assembled from proprietary components supplied from France by Lacoste & Battman and Malicet and Blin. De Dion engines, a range of 6 hp, 9hp, and 10 hp, all of which were of two-cylinder unit construction, were used throughout. The car was nicely furnished in cream lined with gold and appeared to be good value priced at £185.

A local newspaper reporter wrote an account of his visit to Waddington Motors:

Motors in the Making
Visit to a Middlesbrough Factory
Where Cars are Built
The North v. The Midlands

A new industry is growing up in Middlesbrough which makes the iron town a centre of interest to every motorist in the North country. Messrs Waddington and Hall, of Newport Road, have established a motor factory in Greta street, and there is ample prospect that their enterprise will be crowned with success. .For some years this well-known firm have been actively engaged in the fitting, testing, and repairing of motors, but when, some three of four months ago, they branched out into Greta street, they decided to act on the principle that "if a thing is worth doing at all, it is worth doing well from start to finish".Consequently, the new premises were converted into an elaborately equipped factory for the building of motors and motor cars and cycles. This means that the firm make their own parts to their own designs, and by thus attending to the minutest details, are able to guarantee their cars for twelve months against all defects of material and workmanship. The only parts they do not make are castings and car bodies, which mostly come from Midland shops, though one body is now being turned out locally by a Stockton carriage builder. Indeed, as many essentials as possible are obtained from local iron and other firms, and all the brass parts are cast in Middlesbrough. So far, this new development in the industrial world of Teesside has met with gratifying results. A large number of cars and motor bicycles have been built for customers in the district within thirty mile of Middlesbrough, and even more have been turned out to the order of enthusiasts living further afield. The factory is under the personal management of one of the partners in the firm, Mr. Arthur Hall, (assisted by his brother, Mr. E. Hall), through whose courtesy as a representative of the "Herald" was recently given an opportunity of watching.

THE METHODS ADOPTED

The principal types of cars manufactured are those of 12 and 24 horsepower capacity. Much more space would be required and far greater expenseinvolved if the building of an unlimited number of types were undertaken. In thus narrowing their operations, Messrs Waddington and Hall have acted wisely, for it will be readily understood that, by not attempting too much, they are able to turn out in really first-class style what they do take up. None but the best workmen are employed, and these number about 23, local workmen being preferred. There is a well-equipped machine shop driven by four electrical motors - a fifth is now being put down - and stocked with all the latest kind of tools used in motor manufacture, such as machines and tools for planing and shaping, for boring, for drilling and for grinding cams and spindles. The "unmotoric" mind may feel a trifle befogged as to the precise meaning of that queer little word "cam" — though there are even greater mysteries in the motor vocabulary - so it will be best to explain that it is an ingenious arrangement for lifting fhe valves of the motor. On the ground floor there is a roomy garage and a depeartment with apparatus for vulcanising and repairing rubber tyres. Altogether, accommodation is provided for about 50 cars. There are two inspection pits, a blacksmith's shop, and an office, and a large shop is now being prepared for the sole purpose of

ERECTING THE CARS

Upstairs, again, is a pattern-maker's shop and a large store room. Motor car building must not be confused with the manufacture of cycles. There is very little similarity between the methods employed, for motors are so much heavier and stronger that they are built more on the principles of a locomotive. Mssrs. Waddington and Hall have perfected and are adopting a system of their own of high tension magnetic ignition. The electricity is automatically supplied from a generator, which will either charge the accumulators, and store it or ignite the motor itself. Another interesting point explained to the Pressman was in connection with the all- important gearing apparatus. All the gears used are accurately cut by a proper machine, the object being to ensure absolute noiselessness. For the change speed gear a special feature is introduced, there being four speeds and reverse on one lever, and it is possible to change from any one speed to any other without going through any intermediate gear. This is an advantage alone that makes this car unique, and will appeal strongly to all practical motorists. The interlocking and safety apparatus is full of interest. Crank shafts - to come to another point - are of solid steel forgings, and a special point is that the bearings are ample in number and wearing surface. Great care is taken to make every part of the car accessible, the mechanism being easily dismountable. The valves are all mechanically operated, and are on one side of the motor, and the whole of the combustion and valve chambers are water jacketed

THE BEST MAKERS

Always underestimate their motor, and so it will be found in the case of those turned out from tile Middlesbrough factory. Their 12-horse power motor will give 15 on the brake, and their 24 horse power 30. Patriotic motorists who like to feel they are supporting native enterprise will be interested in Mssrs. Waddington and Hall's assurance that their cars are English built and fitted down to the back axle. In this they strike out a new line to some of their predecessors in the trade who have been accustomed to build cars and put French engines into them. At present there are four cars in the making at Greta street - two 24 - horse power four cylinder, and two 12-horse power, two cylinder. The very latest branch of the business is also being followed up. It will be news to many who displayed a keen interest in the Motor Boat Derby across Channel between Calais and Dover to learn that these "wild little demons" can be, and are, made in Middlesbrough Those blessed with a vivid imagination may even picture the turbid waters of the Tees cleaving to the thunderous rush of these marvellous craft in keen competition for some local trophy. Already Mr. Hall has designed and built

A MARINE MOTOR

of 7 horse power, single cylinder, and another of 24 horse power has just been started upon. The one of 7 horse power was for a local gentleman, and as soon as the engines are fitted to the boat, which now lies at a Stockton wharf, it will be seen gaily careering along the river. Mr. Hall introduced into its construction a reversing propeller, which makes it possible to alter the direction of the boat without reversing or stopping the engines. "What of the future?" it may be asked. Can Middlesbrough, can Teesside, can the North generally, rely on a supply of motors made in their own countryside from the best materials, and with the best of workmanship put into them? The particulars given above are surely a complete answer to the query. If Middlesbrough men want motors there is no need for them to give the order to the midlands or to France: they can get it done at home, and have the satisfaction of watching the car growing into shape under their own eyes. For themselves, Messrs. Waddington and Hall have great faith in the development of this latest off-shoot of their enterprise.

AS ENGLISHMEN

They naturally do not like me thought that in 1903 there was an average of £100,000 worth of French cars brought to this country every month. They want to help to bring the trade more into the hands of English firms, and, as there are no other motor factories nearer than Leeds or Glasgow - and those, they contend, not on such thorough lines as the one now established at Middlesbrough - they see no reason why Teesside should not have a branch of an industry, the possibilities of which are unlimited. They also think, and with justice, that there ought to be some patriotism amongst motor car buyers, especially when the manufacturer is willing to guarantee his goods

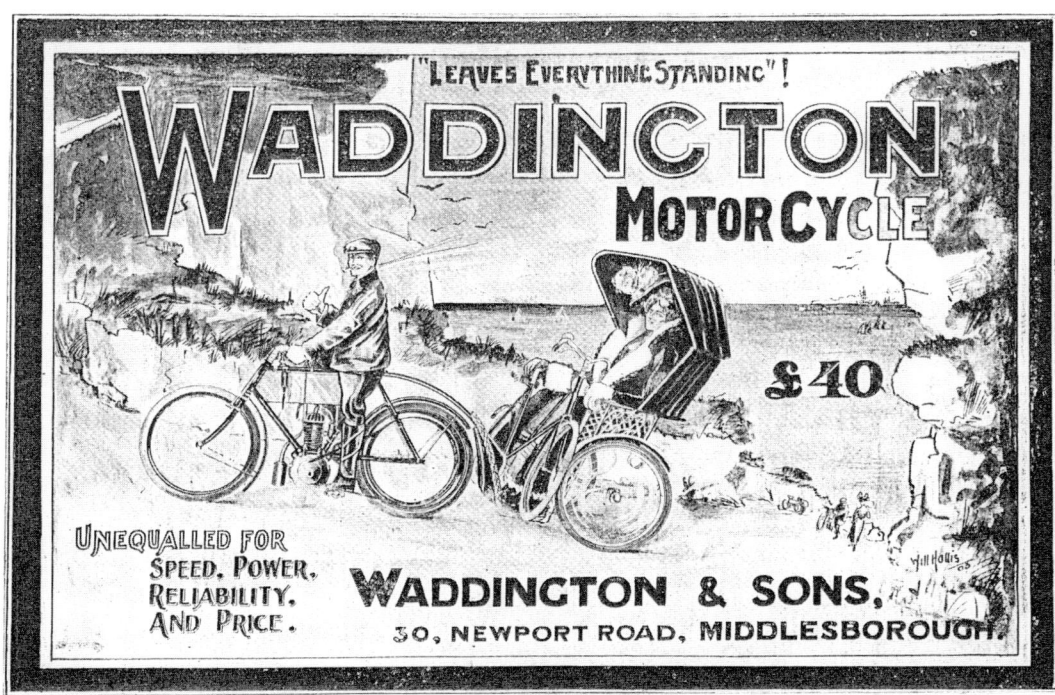

Advertisement for Waddington Motorcylces. *Courtesy of the Vintage Motorcycle Club.*

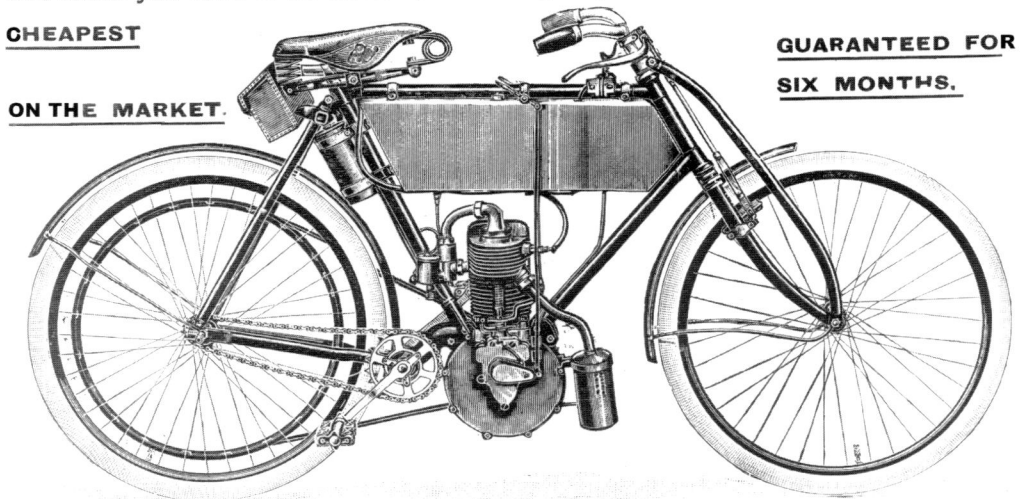

Nothing daunted the early motorist from a century ago. Like these intrepid travellers with this unusual outfit, namely a 1903 2.25hp Jesmond made by the Jesmond Cycle Company of Newcastle on Tyne, towing a wickerwork passenger trailer. It had a Fafnir engine with coil ignition made in Germany and the drive was by belt with a single fixed gear. The photograph is without doubt evocative of a lazy peaceful summer's day in the Edwardian period judging by the name board of Swineshead station in Lincolnshire The couple seem a fair way from home on Teesside? With considerable composure the cameraman, Mr Wilcox, has, with his lady in all her finery assisted by a willing signalman and boy worker, captured a moment in motoring and railway history.
Courtesy Mr M Wilcox

A formal meeting of the Northern League of clubs in 1907 in the committee room of the King's Head Hotel. All have ties on but closer inspection shows one of two gentlemen are still wearing waterproof leggings. Clubs attending were: South Shields, Sunderland, Stockton, Darlington, Bishop Auckland, Durham, Hartlepool, Middlesbrough. Unattached clubs were: Harrogate, Scarborough, Newcastle, Leeds, Bradford and Hull.
Courtesy of Middlesbrough & District Motor Club

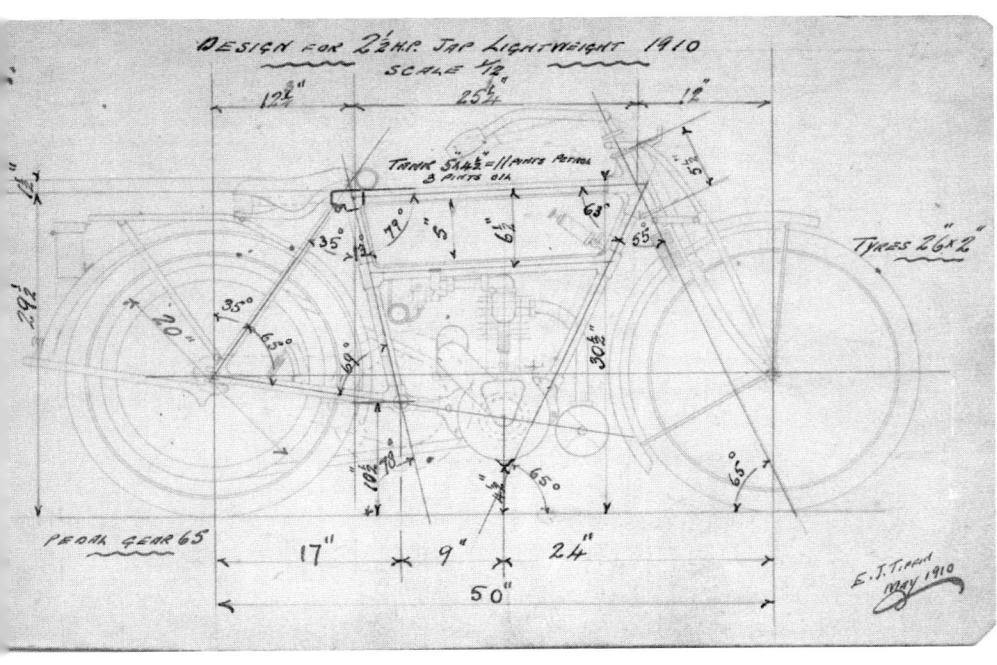

Typical of a cycle shop dealer of the pre-World War One era, Mr Frank Smith of Sunderland used this scale blueprint in 1910 to build a light weight two-and-half horsepower J.A.P. engined machine for local customer Douglas McLaren of Flint Hill Farm. Built to the customer's order and specifications, this motorcycle had single speed pedal-assisted belt drive. Note the added luxury of spring front fork.
Courtesy of John Smith

This splendid car on a splendid royal occasion is at the opening of the Transporter Bridge, Middlesbrough, 17th October 1911. Local pioneer motorist George Scobie Smith has the honour of driving his Royal Highness Prince Arthur of Connaught (in top hat), accompanied by the mayor Sir Hugh Bell (Bart.), to officially open the newly-constructed Transporter Bridge to link the north and south banks of the River Tees. This French-made car of 1907 is a 28 horsepower Delaunay Beauville Landaulette with a four-speed box and chain drive. It was as highly regarded as vehicles by Panhard, Daimler, and Rolls Royce, although not as expensive. Owners of these luxury cars were not normally expected to drive as a chauffeur was engaged for this purpose.

Courtesy of The Dorman Museum, Middlesbrough

In the first decade of the new century cycle dealers throughout the Country were adapting heavyweight cycle frames to accommodate small engines. In 1902 the partnership of Yare & Cobb were just such a firm who operated in Bright St., Middlesbrough. Their machine, shown here, was assembled from proprietary parts, mainly BSA, and was fitted with a Belgian made Minerva engine. Mr Reg Grant, who worked at the firm, together with Mr Cobb produced this machine between them. By 1903 it was sold and later came into the ownership of Mr Ashby of Nunthorpe, registration DC 6. Bert Ashby related many stories of his travels. One such adventure took him to Norfolk to visit a relative. The journey was fraught with problems, mainly drive belt slipping, punctures and even the replacement of an exhaust valve on the roadside, eventually arriving at his destination after three days!

Yare & Cobb's premises in Bright Street, Middlesbrough, where Bert Ashby's bike was built.

One of the popular Club meetings at Marton Bungalow in the early years of the Middlesbrough and District Motor Cycle Club, thought to be in 1907. The gent on the right is founder-member Geoff Liddle.
Courtesy of Middlesbrough and District Motor Club

MIDDLESBROUGH AND DISTRICT MOTOR CLUB

At the Dawn of Teesside Motor Sport the first competitive events on record were confined to motor cycle road reliability trials and petrol consumption tests over various routes around Teesside and Cleveland. Veteran machines, most of which were single speed, direct belt drive, with little or no suspension, could achieve 336 miles to a gallon at an average of 12 miles an hour on the better roads! Another form of competition at that time would be included in club social runs like this one, whereby riders would be stopped at check points along the route and given a task to complete on the machine in a set time, thereby gaining or losing points on their performance.

In October 1905 a meeting of about 40 motorcyclists gathered at Mr Sanderson's home at 105 Linthorpe Road. It was decided to form a club to be known as the Middlesbrough and District Motor Cycle Club. The first secretary was Mr Jeff Liddle, a well-known garage owner in the town. An impressive number of prominent citizens were among the first members of the Club prior to the First World War, including Charles Dorman (Dorman Long and Co.) and L.F. Gjers (Gjers Rolling Mills).

Three weeks after the Club was established it staged its first motor cycle competition, a hill climb. The venue was Ormesby Bank on the outskirts of the town, which had a gradient of 1 in 12 and 1 in 10. The Club's first meeting rooms in the town for social and technical lectures, usually illustrated with lantern slides, were in the Corporation Hotel,. Famous personalities gave lectures, such as James Landsdown Norton, who gave one such presentation focussing on tuning and reliability. Reliability road trials of 100 or 200 miles were often organised and in 1912 the first of many flexibility hill climbs at Yearby Bank near Redcar took place (although it wasn't the first club to run there, as in 1904 the newly-formed Stockton Auto Club promoted a car event there in August of that year).

After the 1914-1918 war it was not long before the Club was up and running again, although the conflict had taken its toll on its former younger members. As a result of developments prompted by the war effort, advances were made in materials and the design technology of the internal combustion engine. This spilled over into civilian life, prompting increased public awareness and the birth of a new interest in motor sport. With the increase in car ownership among the members, it was found by 1921 that the Club needed to change its name to the Middlesbrough and District Motor Club. In the next 20 years, despite the financial depressions during that period, the Club moved forward and in 1926 gained his own permanent premises in Clarendon Road, Middlesbrough.

The First Richmond Meet of 1907. The North Eastern Automobile Association organised the first big meeting place for clubs and fellow enthusiasts of motoring in Richmond, the ancient capital of Swaledale, North Yorkshire, assembling in the market square on Good Friday. No competitive element was involved, other than an award for the largest club attendance, although individual clubs did arrange competitions en route. Clubmen from Durham and as far south as South Yorkshire descended in droves for this first Bank Holiday run of the year, often in atrocious weather on main roads little better than farm tracks which soon became a sea of mud. A strong desire amongst riders was to form the Northern League of clubs. However, with the onset of World War One, all came to no avail and the idea petered out. Nevertheless, many strong bonds of friendship were forged between the new northern clubs for get-togethers in years to come.
Courtesy of Middlesbrough and District Motor Club

Start of the John Gjers Cup 100 mile Reliability Trial.

Bob Richardson (left), local agent for Moto-Reve and well-known jeweller in Middlesbrough, along with Jimmy Gilchrist, taking part in the 1909 petrol consumption trial in which Bob set a new world record of 136 miles to the gallon. Pedalling was allowed. Jimmy Gilchrist is riding a Zenith.

A splendid view of the Cleveland countryside at Castleton Bank Hill Climb, about 1912. Rider of the 2 3/4 hp. Douglas gives instruction to competitor no. 35.
Courtesy of Middlesbrough & District Motor Club

A wet start to the sidecar navigation run assembled outside Middlesbrough Town Hall in the early 1920s.
Courtesy of Middlesbrough & District Motor Club

The camera captures this wonderful period shot of the weigh-in of a Rex motorcycle prior to the Castleton Hill Climb in North Yorkshire, 1912.
Courtesy of Middlesbrough & District Motor Club

Arthur Saltmer taking part in the stop/start test, believed to be at the same event in the Castleton Hill Climb competition, 1912.
Courtesy of Middlesbrough & District Motor Club

Some of the most important events organised by the Club were:

1920s-1950s	Gymkhanas
1921	Saltburn Sand Speed Trial
1936-1955	Sand racing on Coatham Beach, Redcar
1928	Motor Cycle Football, Nationwide
1920s & 1930s	Hill Climbs, Yearby Bank, and Off-road Hill Climbs, Shepherds Hill, Swainby
1936	Ormesby Hall Miniature TT Road Races; Grass Track Races, local venues i.e. Ormesby Cricket Ground and Acklam, extending in post-war years to include Portrack, Stockton and Stewart Park, Middlesbrough.
1938	The famous Scott Trial, Swainby in Cleveland (a joint event organised with Stockton Motor Club)
1940s	Highly successful fund-raising drive for the purchase of a Spitfire for Middlesbrough
1950s	Speedway at Cleveland Park, Middlesbrough. Car Rallies and Navigation Trials
1950s	Scrambles at Hob Hill, at Saltburn. The Cleveland Grand National, later called The Cleveland Trial
1959	Road Races for cars/motorcycles at Thornaby and Croft. Off-road reliability trials for motor cycles throughout the year.

In the late 1950s an RAC /ACU training scheme was set up for learner motorcycle riders to promote road safety, becoming more prominent as the years went on. On the social side, many fund-raising events for charity were set up to benefit under-privileged and handicapped children.

Marton Bungalow Tea Rooms did such good business from the motoring club meets that the owners applied for a license to sell 1 gallon cans of petrol.
Courtesy of Craig Porritt

It is hard to believe that this photograph was taken pre-First World War (1914-18) only five miles outside Middlesbrough. Ponder for a moment to gaze at the leafy lane setting. On the left of the picture a little boy and girl watch as a rider gets a push off by Jeff Liddle. The side car drivers are Henry Fairgrieve and brother John. On the right, the waitress from the Bungalow Cafe holds onto a dog.
Courtesy of Middlesbrough & District Motor Club

Henry Challans making final adjustments to his 1910 3.5 horsepower Premier before the start of a Middlesbrough & District Motor Cycle Club trial. This view at Marton Bungalow corner looks towards Normanby. Note the strip of grass in the centre of the road alongside Stewart Park.
Courtesy of Middlesbrough & District Motor Club

ARMSTRONG WHITWORTH

It is thought that Sir W.G. Armstrong Whitworth of Elswick and Scotswood, known for the manufacture of heavy machinery ordinance and battleships, built a car in 1902. What is certain is that Armstrong Whitworth cars were supplied to the public in 1907. Two types were made, the 15-20 hp and the 25-30 hp. In the year leading up to the First World War, a range of 4-cylinder and 6-cylinder engined cars were produced. Prices ranged from £375 for the 15/20 horsepower model to £850 for the 30/50 horsepower model. Car production ceased in 1914. In 1920 Armstrong-Whitworth merged with Siddley-Deasey, known as the Armstrong-Siddley Group. An early example of a 15/20 was on display at the Museum of Science and Engineering in Newcastle.

CARROW CARS

Advertisement for a Carrow car, priced £525. Carrow Cars Ltd commenced manufacture in Whitley Bay, Newcastle-upon-Tyne in 1919. This very sporty looking light 2-seater was supplied with an 11.9 hp four-cylinder Dorman engine and a three-speed gearbox with a shaft drive. An electric starter was an optional extra. By 1921 the works had been moved to Hanwell, Middlesex and the Carrow was fitted with a 1,795 c.c. Peters engine. Faced with manufacturing difficulties which made it unprofitable to continue to make vehicles, the end of the firm came in 1923.
Courtesy of the Worthington-Williams Collections

THE GOLDEN FORD

A NOVEL END-ON EFFECT.
Mr. A. E. George on his "Golden" Ford, which achieved great success at Saltburn.

Mr. N. Tucket in the driving seat of the Golden Ford. George and Joblin were a large northern Ford agent in the pre-World War One years with depots in most big towns, including Newcastle and Darlington. Mr George was a good salesman with an eye for publicity. On its inception in 1908 the Ford Model 'T' was the first mass produced people's car and the first car to have a detachable cylinder head. Mr George also noted (although not intended by Ford) that it could be mildly tuned and used for racing. This he did, his 'Golden' Ford being fitted with a magnificent-looking streamlined body made in brass. One of his first sales pitches was at The Saltburn Speed Trials in 1911 where he had a great success. In recent years the car became a topic of media interest when TV company 'Wall-to-Wall' filmed a restoration rebuilt with the 'Salvage Squad' and much help through Tucket Bros., the noted 'T' Ford specialists.

ANGUS-SANDERSON

This nicely restored 1920 car was made by Angus-Sanderson in Birtley, the same firm that made the N.U.T motorcycle, when Hugh Mason became connected with Angus Sanderson. It was a well-built, quality car with a two-and-a-quarter litre side valve four-cylinder Taylor engine with detachable head and Rigley 3-speed gearbox. It had a top speed of 40-50 mph and could do 25 miles per gallon. However, like many other car manufacturers after World War One, the firm were too slow to fulfil orders due to non-delivery of individual parts from outside suppliers. Would-be owners had to wait 12 months or more, resulting in many orders being cancelled.
Courtesy of Maurice Jennings

BLACK PRINCE (THE NINE-DAY WONDER)

Barnard Castle, County Durham, was almost at the source of the River Tees and the furthest north of Teesside motor manufacturers. Businessman Mr Ernest Waisby and Mr. Cameron, who lived in Askern, had distinctly unconventional ideas when it came to designing motor cycles and cycle cars. Their design for the Black Prince motorcycle was strikingly futuristic for its time and, in its design, they seemed to be making life as difficult as possible for themselves. The British motorist has always been conservative in his taste and after the First World War even more so. They started with a pressed steel frame of which the tank was to be an integral part. The engine was a fore-and-aft mounted horizontal twin two-stroke and transmission was through a two-speed gearbox and chain primary drive which terminated with a shaft final drive. Wheels were fully enclosed pressings for easy cleaning. In fact the whole machine was way ahead of its time. Their Black Prince appeared at the Olympia show in 1919 but it was not complete and it is unknown if even a single model was ever sold!
Courtesy of the Worthington Williams Collection

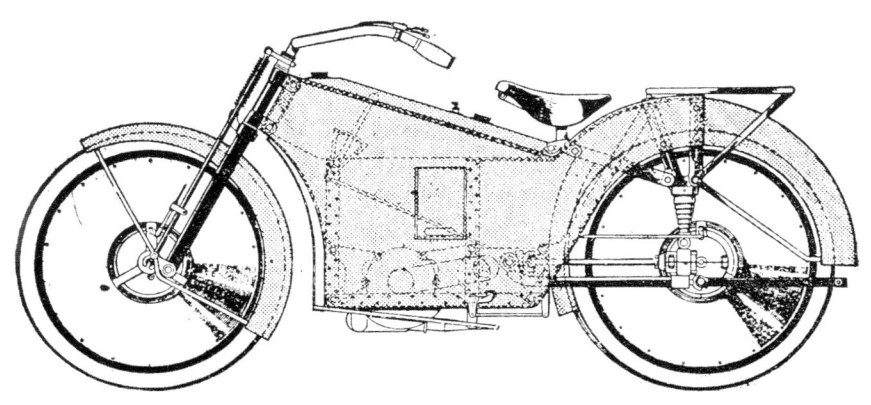

We know for certain that one or possibly two Black Prince cycle cars were built as one is now on show in the Bowes Museum, Barnard Castle. The B.P. Cycle Car, as it was known, is now rather laughable and I would imagine, even in 1919, anyone looking for economic transport would have given it a wide berth. It is crude, to say the least, fitted with a two-stroke, 3 horsepower engine, or alternatively with two single-cylinder two-stroke engines fitted together, giving a total capacity of 670 c.c., or 6 horsepower, driving through a two-speed gearbox, all fitted in an ash chassis. At £125, one could have made a better choice. By 1921, Black Prince Motors Ltd, at Thorngate Mills, Barnard Castle, had ceased to exist.
Courtesy of the Worthington Williams Collection

THE CLEVELAND MOTOR CYCLE COMPANY 1912 MIDDLESBROUGH

Egerton Price, local builder and developer who became Mayor of Middlesbrough in 1922, was a motor enthusiast as well as a visionary. Like several other North-East businessmen, he could see a bright future for the small motor cycle manufacturer. Unfortunately it happened at the wrong time, being only two years before World War One, which stalled what could have been developed into a promising small enterprise given a fair chance.

Egerton built his first motor cycle in 1912, which was one of only 10 ever made. The bikes were assembled in the workshops in Douglas Street, Middlesbrough and he had the name 'Cleveland' formed into the casting of the magneto timing cover. Most of the parts, such as frame-lugs, were bought in from B.S.A. in Birmingham. The engine was a 'Green Precision', available in several different horsepower ratings. The three-speed rear hub was supplied by Sturmey Archer. All the enamelling and nickel plating was probably carried out by Yare and Cobb in Bright Street. The final paintwork, tank and lining of the wheel rims was carried out by 'Con' Rogers in his Linthorpe workshops.

Egerton Price had enormous confidence in his assembled product. Not only did he take part in many local and national hill climbs, including the famous Edinburgh run, but he persuaded a 22 year-old Stockton lad by the name of Fred Dixon to ride the Cleveland in the 1914 Isle of Man TT races. Regrettably, due to a difference of opinion as to how the machine was to be prepared, the bike was not up to the task in hand, and young Freddy retired after two laps with several stops for drive belt replacement and also magneto problems. This was the beginning of Freddy Dixon's TT racing career, which eventually took him to stardom in the years to come. In the post World-War One period Egerton was unable to compete in the motor cycle manufacturing market and his pre-war enterprise declined.

Manufacturer and rider Egerton Price photographed on one of his machines for his sales brochure in 1912.
Courtesy of Reg Price

Bicycles & Motors Wanted or For Sale.

CLEVELAND MOTOR CYCLES AND SIDE CARS,
"THE BEST THAT YOU CAN BUY."

3½ and 4¼ h.p. SINGLE CYLINDERS, fitted with Sturmey-Archer Three Speeds.
IDEAL FOR SIDE-CAR WORK.
WILL CLIMB ANY HILL.
Made by
THE CLEVELAND MOTOR CYCLE CO.,
DOUGLAS-ST., MIDDLESBROUGH.
WHOLESALE ONLY.

Local Agent: G. CARTER, Motor Engineer LINTHORPE, MIDDLESBROUGH.
Agents Wanted where not Represented.
Send for Lists.

Advertisement for the Cleveland Motor Cycle Company
Courtesy of Reg Price

Egerton Price demonstrating the Cleveland's reliability at Yearby Bank Hill Climb, 1913.
Courtesy of Reg Price

Showroom for the smart Egerton Price Cleveland Motor Cycle Co., 235 Linthorpe Road, Middlesbrough, from 1912 until 1914, displaying the 4 hp green Precision-engined machine, priced at 50 guineas, which was a small fortune for the working man at the time.

Advertisment for William Armstong, Motor Agent, Linthorpe Road, Middlesbrough, from the Motor Club Journal, June 1936. The firm was founded in 1897 as a cycle dealer.

By 1913 racing cars were taking on a more streamlined shape. This Straker Squire, is being driven by R.S. Witchell, the winner of his class at 86.9 mph, at Saltburn. These early meetings were organised by the Yorkshire Auto Club.
Courtesy of Mr T R Nicholson

Note the difference in the frontal area of this 1908 Itala, driven by Mr Wil-de-Gose at Saltburn Speed trials in 1911. The car was owned by H.Young, the Brewery family.
Courtesy of Bridget Laycock

Scott Works riders Clarry Wood and Harry Langdon, winners of the 1922 sidecar race, Saltburn. The girl in the photo could be well-known lady speedway rider Dot Cowley or one of the secretaries of the Scott works. The other chap on her left is Ernie Mainwaring.
Courtesy of Middlesbrough & District Motor Club

A small section of the 60,000 crowd which stretched for about two miles between Saltburn to Marske in the early years of the Yorkshire Auto Club's speed trials.

ROWLAND WINN

A smartly dressed Rowland Winn at the wheel of his Rakish Model T Ford Special, July 1911, his full attention focussed on the cameraman, he seems unaware of the approaching car. This location outside of the Alexandra Hotel in Saltburn was a popular spot for many the car drivers taking part in the speed trials to pose for the camera. Rowland Winn, motoring pioneer and Lord Mayor of Leeds in 1938, was one of a small group of Northern motorists who fought a protracted campaign against the 12 mph speed limit. As a member of the Yorkshire Auto Club he competed in the Saltburn Speed Trials on his Model T Ford Special.

In later years Winn's other interests included sailing his yacht Lily Maud moored at Bridlington. On weekend visits he was installing a Cadillac engine into the yacht when he became friendly with Aircraftsmen SHAW (Lawrence of Arabia). Shaw's work while stationed at Bridlington was supervising the fitting out and testing of the armour-plated target boats. In free time the two sailed together.

ELDRIDGE:
MEPHISTOPHELES THE FIAT EX-GRAND PRIX CAR.

Ernest Eldridge was the son of a London money lender and was educated at Harrow, where he acquired his qualifications as an engineer. Motor racing became his passion and, using his Father's wealth, he indulged himself in a life-style of a playboy, acquiring a reputation as a bit of a womaniser, both at home and abroad.

The Fiat was rebuilt on a lengthened (18') chassis using frame rails cut from a London bus. Eldridge fitted a war-surplus Fiat A1Z B15 six-cylinder aero engine: 21,706cc; four valves per cylinder; 320b.h.p. at 1,800 r.p.m. Whilst taking part in record attempts in France in 1924 he took the World Speed Record for the Flying Kilometre at 146.01 mph., throwing a tyre tread in the process. In the same year, fearless Eldridge, competing at Saltburn against arch rival Malcolm Campbell in his Sunbeam, attained the speed of 135.7m.p.h.

Now that these speeds had been achieved it was virtually impossible to safely continue further world record attempts between Saltburn and Marske as it logically requires a longer stretch of suitable beach to obtain higher speeds. It was claimed by the drivers that a total of 6 miles of reasonably smooth beach without the piers would be needed - three miles to build up speed before entering the measured kilometre and a further 2 miles for slowing down.

Ernest Eldridge outside the Alexandra Hotel, Saltburn, in the 21,706 cc six-cylinder Fiat. This Fiat-based monster of a car was born in 1907 from a Grand Prix chassis. In 1908 it was raced at Brooklands by Felice Nazzaro using a S.B.4 Corsa 18,146cc engine, with Nazzaro lapping at 126mph. The car then changed owners and eventually, after WW1 and an engine blow up, it was bought by Ernest Eldridge for £25. His fearless style of driving was a serious threat to Sir Malcolm Campbell's dominance of the Speed Trials in 1924.

Alf Kirby, who worked for the Tees and Hartlepool Port Authority, was a keen motorcyclist and amateur photographer. He took many photos on his runs out into the Cleveland countryside on his faithful Rudge Multi of 1913. This photograph records a run out to Helmsley in 1921, which had to be abandoned at Newgate Bank due to belt drive slip. In spite of this disappointment, a roadside picnic is in progress in true Romany style, with kettle on a stick over a fire, making a fun day out for his three sons, Alf on the bike, and on the wall Jimmy (left) and George (right).
Courtesy of Alf Kirby

Mrs Kirby sits quite contentedly in the basket side car near Busby Hall on the Stokesley and Calton Road. Note the unmade road with the grass growing in the middle. The faithful old Rudge served the Kirby family for many years.
Courtesy of Alf Kirby

A relaxed crowd await the next rider up the hill on Yearby Bank near Redcar, probably at a Middlesbrough and District Motor Club event of 1923. The big chap in the leather coat smiling at the camera is Manchester Work's D.O.T. race co-ordinator, Percy Butler, who was owner of the Dreadnought Insurance Company. The machine just visible in the foreground is an oil-cooled D.O.T. Bradshaw, probably ridden by Works D.O.T. rider Peter Bell. Manufacturers derived much publicity from this type of local club event.

Hutchinson from York on a Sunbean at the 1923 Yearby Bank Hill Climb. Note the scar on his head from a previous crash. This appears to be a practice run as no crash hat is worn.

HILL CLIMBS

The first recorded hill climb in the area was organised by Stockton Automobile Club in 1904 at Yearby Bank near Redcar. Staged over 1174 yards, the fastest time of the day was made by Mr A Hall, in a 20 hp. Waddington and Hall automobile at a speed of 13.95 mph. It is pure speculation, but could it have been the Waddington car manufactured in Middlesbrough on Newport Road. Second place was taken by Leonard Ropner on a 12 hp. Napier.

From the very early beginnings of motor sport, hill climbs have been a regular part of the Club's calendar. Close behind the Stockton Club was the newly-formed Middlesbrough Motor Cycle Club, which staged its first hill climb on Ormesby Bank in 1905. In 1919, in conjunction with the York and District Motor Cycle Club, Middlesbrough Club held an Open Hill Climb on Sutton Bank near Thirsk. Even the Hartlepool Primrose League Motor Club crossed the River Tees to stage an event on Yearby Bank early in 1920.

Many more small club hill climbs were staged within the period between the First World War and 1925, with some clubs staging as many as six in one year. Sadly in 1925, due to police and the governing motor sport bodies raising objections, most of the officially organised public road hill climbs in the area were abandoned - reasons being the increase in public transport traffic and the urbanisation of the area, although it is recorded that some other clubs staged impromptu events at Rosedale Chimney into the 1930s.

This was not the end of hill climbing on Teesside as, by the mid-1930s, events were staged at off-road venues, for example the Shepherds Hill events outside the village of Swainby in Cleveland. Included in the programme at the Shepherds Hill event were classes for cars and solo motorcycles, run on a knockout basis. Later, circuit racing was introduced, which today would be better described as 'scrambling'.

Rosedale Hill Climb, 1927
Courtesy of Alf Kirby

Miles Fulford, sidecar manufacturer and competitor, at Rosedale Chimney Hill Climb. These early wickerwork body sidecars were extremely flexible, giving the passenger a small degree of comfort.
Courtesy of Wallace Holmes

Henry Hodson of Leeds took part in many North East speed events during the Twenties and Thirties in his own car, which he manufactured in a small factory in Leeds. It was primarily marketed as a racing car but sports and sports/touring versions were later produced. The car was powered by a side-valve, 1,496 cc Anzani engine, which drove through a four-speed gearbox. The racing version was reputed to do 100mph when supercharged and even the sports version was capable of 90 mph. Not many Hodgson cars were sold in the south of England, most sales being mainly concentrated in Yorkshire. The Hodson competed in many Teesside events and became a new force in sprint hill climb and sand racing.
Courtesy of Middlesbrough & District Motor Club

MOTOR CYCLE FOOTBALL

Introduced in 1924 by its originator Bill Ryan, Yorkshire Centre President, the game was run under A.C.U. Rules of six-a-side, using an Association-sized ball, and played 15 minutes each way. The game was introduced in the North East but spread rapidly throughout the country. There was no shortage of clubs eager to play the new game and a league system was soon introduced, with keen competition between the clubs. Accidents were inevitable, but it seemed to be more the machines than the riders which came off worst.

The Middlesbrough Club received an invitation to play a game down at Camberley, with Middlesbrough, the victors, receiving a silver challenge cup. Other matches were played with local clubs throughout the season. For example, Middlesbrough played Scarborough on Scarborough sands and they played the Hartlepool Primrose League on Seaton Sands. The Stockton and Darlington Clubs followed and the following year became a boom year for the game, with clubs playing at Tadcaster, the British Legion at Thirsk, Barnard Castle Unionist Club, and a Thirsk YMCA. That year, Middlesbrough played Cumberland County at Stockton, with Middlesbrough winning a resounding 15-nil. The second match was played against Grimsby Motor Cycle and Car Club at Samuelson's Athletic Ground, Middlesbrough, with Middlesbrough winning that too! However, triumph was short-lived. They reached the final and played Coventry at Crystal Palace where, due to heavy rain, the match was abandoned. The replay, staged at Headingley on 20th March 1927, found Middlesbrough being trounced by 11 goals to 1.

The Middlesbrough team which played Ripon. Seated on machines (left to right): Albert Smith, Walter Creasor, Frank Dixon, Bill Collinson, Fred Creasor, Phil Blake. Standing: Alf Armstrong and Alf Buttress.
Courtesy of Middlesbrough & District Motor Club

The Middlesbrough Club team seem to have lost control of the ball to Ripon, while Fred Creasor bites the dust and Frank Dixon, centre, looks on anxiously.
Courtesy of Middlesbrough & District Motor Club

RONNIE PARKINSON

No record of Teesside motor sports would be complete without some of Ronnie Parkinson's exploits being related since he achieve a high level of fame in the motor cycle racing world.

In his sand racing career he established an impressive record: At Saltburn the 350 cc 20 mile championship (1928-30), the 500 cc in 1932 and the 1000 cc in 1932; the Scottish 20 mile championship in 1928; the Daily Mail 20 Mile Speed Championship at Pendine in 1928; the Southport 50 mile 500 cc and Unlimited Championships. He held three Southport Gold Star Awards for exceeding 100 miles per hour. The list goes on and, in total, it amounted to 360 firsts throughout his racing career. Not only a sand racing expert, he did ride in the amateur TT known as the Manx Grand Prix, five times riding his AJS. His best place was in 1927 when he finished fifteenth. Known for his skills as an engine tuner, he worked as mechanical superintendent at Hackney Wick Speedway Stadium on an extremely high wage, plus a bonus on the team's results. He also looked after the Wimbledon Team machines. He later went to work at Associated Motorcycles, Plumstead, in charge of experimental and engine testing. Whilst working there, he was responsible for the work involving the building and development of the first supercharged four-cylinder V-AJS which developed 50 brake horsepower and was capable of speeds of 100 mph plus. It was tested at Brooklands, where it failed to achieve its desired performance, and required further development. The Second World War intervened and afterwards, whilst working in London, Ronnie became interested in rallying and was offered a choice to drive in the 1949 Alpine Rally in a Bristol Works Car alongside a Czech driver, M. Treybal.

Ron Parkinson, "The White Devil of Pendine", in his specially tailored overalls, proudly displays his works racing 1931 500 cc OHC. S10 model A.J.S. *Courtesy of Ian Denny*

All went well in the early stages of the Rally until reaching Cortina in the Dolomites. A hose blew so a stop was necessary in a small village to undertake temporary repairs. This amounted to wrapping insulating tape around the offending rubber hose and a start was then made to rejoin the rally. However, tragedy struck whilst rounding a hairpin bend on the narrow mountain road. The Bristol skidded on the loose surface and the back wheel struck a road marker. Treybal, driving, lost control and the car shot over the side, somersaulting into a ravine 200 feet below. Miraculously, Treybal was thrown clear and sustained only minor injuries. Ronnie was still in the car when members of the Italian Army found them. It was fortunate for them that the army was holding an exercise in the area, otherwise no-one else witnessed the incident. The pair were rushed to hospital in old Bolzana, where Ron was found to have a depressed skull, caused by a projection on the spare wheel carried in the back seat, which struck him on the head in the fall. Also, his left leg was fractured in four places. After several weeks in hospital in Bolzana, he was flown home to England and up to Thornaby in a private air ambulance. After a long convalescence, Ron returned to full health and then opened a garage business in Bottomley Street, Middlesbrough, and later moved to Eastbourne Road.

A 2-litre 402 drophead Bristol at Croft in 1950, similar to the car driven by Parkinson in 1949 when he was in his Alpine Rally accident.
Courtesy of Jack Wright

FRED DIXON: PORTRAIT OF A LEGEND

Much has been written about Freddy Dixon's life in motor sport racing, most of which is of his exploits and involvement racing Riley's at Brookland. I am sure that many more pages could be written on his exploits racing abroad and also his development work as a consultant when he retired from active motor racing in 1936, but that is beyond the scope of this book.

It is generally assumed that Freddy was a Yorkshireman and hailed from Middlesbrough, but in fact he was born in Stockton on Tees, County Durham, in 1892. Now, almost 50 years after his death in 1956, the stories about Fred have become motoring legend among motor and motoring enthusiasts. As well as his ill-fated TT ride on the Cleveland in 1912, his involvement with local motorcycle sport started in 1910, when he took part in several sprints and hill climbs, instantly gaining himself a reputation as a man of speed, and building up a list of successes. This was prior to him being called up for the army, where he served in motor transport, and rose to the rank of staff sergeant. After his demob from the Army in 1918, he set up the motor engineering and sales business, known as Park Garage, Linthorpe, Middlesbrough, with agencies for Riley and Singer cars and Douglas motor cycles, amongst others.

Here on Teesside, he is best remembered for his racing successes and particularly for his invention of the banking sidecar, the preliminary sketches for which were drawn out in chalk on the garage floor. Fred and Walker Denny, as passenger, won the first Isle of Man T.T. sidecar race on this in 1923. In later years he went on to win the Ulster T.T. on the Ards circuit, in a works-built 1 litre Riley.

Of course he had a string of wins at Brooklands, both in cars and solo and sidecar motorbikes, as well as a whole host of achievements which spanned the years 1910-1936. Not only was he a brilliant and fearless rider, but also he will be remembered for his development work on carburation (always using one carb per cylinder). He is thought to have been the first person to use disk brakes, which he designed and built himself. In September 1932 Fred built his own single seat Racing Riley 9, which he named the Red Mongrel, in his Middlesbrough workshops. Working with his loyal mechanic, Walter Maidens, over several lengthy all-night sessions, finalising the car in the early morning the day before practising started at Brooklands. Fully loaded in the car, they set out on a long drive down the old winding A1 Great North Road, arriving late on Friday night, almost drunk from lack of sleep. On race day he had a very successful run, taking six international records, before setting off back to Teesside, arriving back home early Monday morning completely exhausted.

This 'devil-may-care' character, who cared little for the establishment (his interpretation of rules were that they are made to be bent) never wore goggles while racing. When new rules made it compulsory to have eye protection Fred would arrive on the start line wearing goggles with no lenses. Throughout his racing career he bucked convention, thinking nothing of working all night preparing for a race and expecting all others, Walter Maidens and Len Ainsley, both riding mechanics with him, to do the same. He was a man of complex character, with frequent swings of mood change. The boy apprentices working at Park Garage recall tales of Fred having little patience and he was known to throw hammers at them. It is obvious that he was a man who didn't suffer fools gladly and expected 12 hours work from an eight-hour day. Only a dedicated few stayed to work at the Garage but, strangely, considered it a privilege to work for him.

The day-to-day management of the garage, showrooms and stores was carried out by Frank Dixon, Fred's brother, who, it might be stated, was a very capable motorcycle racing rider in his own right

Fred Dixon with his bike, No.34, "Cleveland".
Courtesy of the Keig Collection

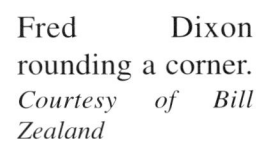

Fred Dixon rounding a corner.
Courtesy of Bill Zealand

Fred Dixon signing autographs at a meeting at Sutton Bank, North Yorkshire
Courtesy of Bill Zealand

The penalty of fame! The ever popular Freddie Dixon run to earth by admiring autograph hunters, after a North Country meeting.

but was overshadowed by his brother's successes. Time and time again, during pre-race preparation, Fred would work for days and nights, snatching two-minute dozes at intervals of 12 hours or more. Fred was small in stature and built like an ox, with a constitution as hard as Dorman Long iron. An incident at Donington Park illustrates this. Fred caught a man helping himself to the toolbox in the paddock. Fred rushed over, lifted him bodily off the ground, threw him over the paddock fence and calmly walked back to continue his work on his Riley. His attention to detail was fanatical. He had his own ideas, no matter how unconventional, which he stuck rigidly to. For instance, in his motorcycle racing days, while the rest of the TT riders used footrest and throttle levers, Fred would fit foot boards and twists grips. Also, he used a small windscreen which he crouched behind, enabling him to dispense with goggles, which he disliked.

One of the best tales I heard was when Fred came home after a weekend of successful racing. He and some friends went out on the town, Fred driving a big open American Essex car. It was suggested by Fred that at the first pub stop the last one out of the car and into the pub would buy everybody a drink. It was agreed by the passengers (laughingly) thinking that Fred, being the driver, was bound to be buying the first round. However, as the open-topped car swept into the gravel car-park, still motoring, Fred smartly stood up onto the driving seat and leapt out of the car and ran into the pub, leaving the rest of his friends and passengers to wrestle with the steering wheel and to bring the car under control to a safe rest. Needless to say, his friends needed double whiskeys all round to settle their shattered nerves, while Fred enjoyed his favourite Pimms. It's not recorded who paid for the round but this is the type of over-exuberant behaviour Fred indulged in. Fred obviously believed that you worked hard and played hard too!

This behaviour didn't go unnoticed by the local police and, after being involved in a drink driving offence in 1935, he was charged and sentenced to six months imprisonment in Durham Prison. There his presence was immediately appreciated by the Governor, who immediately employed him in the Prison Garage, servicing and tuning up police cars which, it might be said, went a darn sight faster afterwards thanks to Freddy's expertise!

In 1934 Fred desired to make an attempt on the British Empire Land Speed Record and bought the ex- works World record 30 foot-long Sunbeam Silver Bullet. When the car arrived on Teesside by rail it was towed up to the rear of Linthorpe Park Garage. As can be imagined, it caused a great deal of speculation and interest among the public. However, when this huge, sleek Sunbeam arrived it was found that with having little or no steering lock it seemed impossible to manoeuvre the car to get a straight push into the garage. Everyone involved stood back and scratched their heads for a solution to the problem. It is said that Fred got one of his workshop lads to bring a five-gallon drum of old engine oil which he then proceeded to pour over the cobbled area so that the back wheels could be swept sideways while the front remained stationary All hands slid the mammoth car round in an arc to line it up with the garage workshop entrance and thence straight in. Simple when you think of it!

Of course, locals thought Fred would have had a few tests of the car on Redcar or Saltburn beach, where the record stood at 135 miles an hour, but it was thought that the local beach was too short a distance for test runs. In any case, it would have to be at Pendine Sands in Wales, where all the British records were attempted, and as the World record stood at 203 miles an hour and was constantly going up, Fred decided to shelve the project and later sold the car.

The winning HRD team outside the Queens Hotel, Isle of Man, 1927. Fred Dixon, with his arm round the shoulder of his wife, Dolly, is to the right of the winning 350 cc H.R.D. machine. Howard Davies is to the left of the bike. A number of other T.T. racing men, surrounded by many Teesside supporters, can be spotted at this celebration party, including: Walter Denny (front row left, standing); Alec Bennett (next seated) and Jimmy Simpson.
Courtesy of Bill Hutton

Fred Dixon, in the driving seat, takes delivery of the Sunbeam Silver Bullet from the works in Wolverhampton, 1934. The lady striding out, on right, is his wife, Dolly, (nee Thew) from Middlesbrough. The man behind her pushing on the wheel is Walter Maidens, Fred's loyal mechanic.
Courtesy of Julian Mazoob

Freddie Dixon, T.T. winner, Brooklands star and tuning wizard, drew this cartoon and sent it to his friends in celebration of his release from 'His Majesty's pleasure' following a short stretch for a motoring offence. Iron man Freddy considered that the road user was mercilessly persecuted by the police, whilst 'real' villains made off unhindered - hence the two toughs in a street brawl causing a public disturbance and the thief making his getaway with a turkey, unseen by the two bobbies busy measuring up the licence plate on the cads motor! Meanwhile Freddie greets his family at the prison gates with the comment 'So this is progress!' Just 70 years on is there any similarity we wonder?

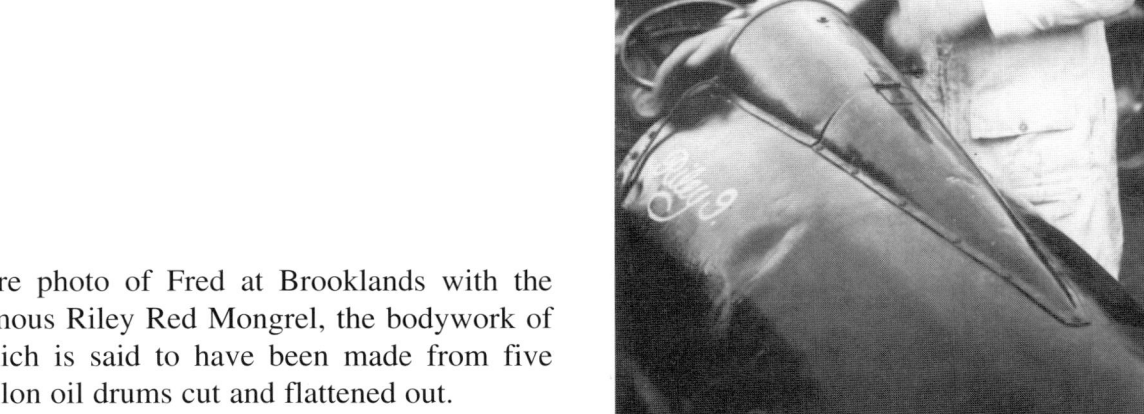

Oh Yes, 1935 is Out—SO AM I!
I believe I am going to have a Happy New Year, and I wish you and yours the same, and all the best for '36!

FREDDIE DIXON
93 Cambridge Road,
　Linthorpe. Middlesbrough.

Rare photo of Fred at Brooklands with the famous Riley Red Mongrel, the bodywork of which is said to have been made from five gallon oil drums cut and flattened out.
Courtesy of Ian Denney

Alf Buttress on a 600cc Panther motorcycle and sidecar.
Courtesy of Middlesbrough & District Motor Club

Alf Buttress, Secretary of Middlesbrough and District Motor Club, known to his colleagues as Alf, but called Freddy at home. Alf joined the club in 1920 and the following year won four trials. He started on a 2/34 Douglas but later transferred his affections to P & M. He was amazingly successful in the sport. In fact Alf accumulated a whole host of trophies and prizes. His most notable successes include the Club's John Gjers Cup in 1921 and in 1925 the Bill Ryan Cup. He went on to compete in the York to Edinburgh, finishing the best solo, and in 1927 he finished the best sidecar. Alf was elected General Secretary in 1923. Apart from his club life, Alf worked as structural engineer and was the River Superintendent with the Tees Conservancy Commission. Away from work his life was the Middlesbrough Motor Club and motor sport in general, serving on the board of the East Yorkshire Centre of the A.C.U. for many years. Much of the club's success over 50 years was due to Alf - the driving force.

Alf Buttress on a Douglas.
Courtesy of Middlesbrough & District Motor Club.

Even on dank, wet and murky days, Ormesby Bungalow Garage and Tea Rooms had a charm of its own. With its mock-Tudor façade, it projects the motoring image of the pre-war period, when a garage owner could give motorists a choice of six different brands of petrol and personal service with a smile.
Courtesy of Craig Poritt.

Liddle's Filling Station, Acklam Road, Middlesbrough.

Famous lady rider, Marjorie Cottle, speeding up Raise Hill in the Travers Trophy trial. Conditions for this event look far from perfect. The ladies in the crowd give Marjorie an encouraging smile and wave her on her way.
Courtesy of Bob Light

Two of the girls out for a spin with their boyfriends on Whit Bank Holiday in 1930. The pub is the Chequers in Dalton Village-on-Tees. The girl on the left is Vera Sinclair on the new Hudson with her best friend, Minnie Pinkney on a two-stroke Levis - in later years to become my mother-in-law!

Interesting photographs of a club trial. Close inspection reveals that the checkpoint is in the High Street of the village of Osmotherley, just off the A 19. Rider number 7 is on a mid-30s A.J.S. Clubmans model. Note the knobbly front tyre which was the trend at the time. The policeman on the left is probably the local area mounted patrol officer. The village scene is virtually unchanged today.
Courtesy of the Evening Gazette, Middlesbrough

The end to a perfect day and extremely evocative of a pre-war era club trial, at what looks like the sheep wash, Swainby-in-Cleveland, with the moorland backdrop. The un-made narrow road winds away to Osmotherley, and some interesting cars can be picked out, including Morris 8s and the local trader vans. The spectators' dress is interesting and riders, in full-length leather coats with thigh-length waders, will raise a smile for modern-day riders. The riders taking advantage of the running stream to wash the mud from their machines, which are Triumph Tiger Eighties with a 350cc BSA in between.
Courtesy of Middlesbrough and District Motor Club

The staple diet of most local clubs has always been the one day sporting trial. Here, at one of the many reliability trials held by the Middlesbrough & District Motor Club in the 1930's, Alex Hill of Harrogate comes out of the fog on his Scott at Church House Bank, Test Hill, Danby Dale.
Courtesy of Middlesbrough Motor Club.

A bright, frosty morning is perfect for such a winter trial, believed to be at Carlton/Swainby, Cleveland, in 1952. Rex Richardson, No.11, is on a B.S.A. No. 13 is Derek Smith and No. 18 is Harold Whiley on an Excelsior. Other bikes are Norton and Matchless.
Courtesy of Newsquest (North East Ltd.)

Ormesby Hall, on the outskirts of Middlesbrough, was a perfect venue for the Middlesbrough Club to stage its first attempt at road racing. Colonel Pennyman, owner of the estate, gave permission to use the main drive and pathways around the manor house to stage racing in 1936. Many well-known northern riders took part, including Jack & Charlie Brett and Denis Parkinson. The Club's up-and-coming star, Gilly Bensley, seen here at the opening meeting on 5th September, running and bump-starting his Norton International, stole the show by winning the Ormesby Handicap. Only one or two events were staged at the Hall before the Second World War and in recent years the club resurrected the venue to stage a number of vintage sprints.

The sun casts a shadow over the final event of the day and the final meeting at Ormesby Hall. The No.4 Velocette rider gets away first. Machines 21 and 22 are Douglas machines, whilst No. 17 appears to be a Rudge.

GRASS TRACK RACING

Despite the high unemployment of the early 1930s, the Teesside clubs soldiered on, be it with falling numbers in club memberships and some events had to be cancelled through lack of entries. However, the Middlesbrough clubs staged several grass track meetings within the town's boundaries at Lane End Farm and Sicklings Farm, Acklam. Both of these meetings were easily accessible for the public, with a bus stop opposite Acklam Garage, and a good crowd of 3000 were rewarded by some thrilling racing. Local man Frank Hodgson showed his early talents on the oval track, racing to win the Acklam Handicap Race on an Aerial. Edgar Kendrew, another local from Stockton, managed third place in the Junior Scratch Race. Bill Kitchen, from Galgate, Lancaster, later to become so popular on the speedway as Wembley captain, won the Senior Scratch Race. Grass racing became such an attraction that many small country show organisers included racing after the show on the long summer nights. In the 1950s Richmond Meet was a favourite annual event, Kilburn Fete another, all supported by Teesside riders.

A warm summer's day in 1947 enjoyed by a large crowd in Stewart Park, Middlesbrough, for this one-off event organised by Middlesbrough and District Motor Club. Marton Hall, sadly no longer there, provided an imposing and impressive backdrop. Keith Betton, on a Triumph nearest the camera, battles it out with Rex Young, BSA, in this 350cc race, with Rex being the eventual winner.
Courtesy of Rex Young

The tapes fly up and they are off at the start of the 500cc race at Stewart Park, Middlesbrough. Again, Rex Young came out the winner.
Courtesy of Rex Young

Excellent action shot showing two unknown riders, one, on the outside, on a speedway Rudge/J.A.P. machine about to be overtaken on the inside by a leg-trailing Speedway Douglas. In post-war years the Middlesbrough and District Motor Club bought its own land at Portrack, and staged many successful events there.

An AJS flat tanker of the late 20s vintage, on the outside, stays ahead of a mid-thirties Norton. It is difficult to say where the photograph was taken. It could be Greatham Airport, Elwick, or the 'Island' Portrack-on-Tees, in the early post-World War Two years.

Frontispiece of the official programme for Hartlepool & District Motor Club's motor-cycle races at Greatham Airport, 1947.

Hartlepools & District Motor Club

Affiliated to A.C.U. through Yorkshire Centre
Associated with the R. A. C.

President : Alderman M. Bloom.
Hon. Sec: S. Killingbeck, 77, Grange Road, West Hartlepool

MOTOR-CYCLE
GRASS TRACK RACES

Restricted Invitation Permit from Yorks Centre A.C.U. No. D.295

GREATHAM AIRPORT
Sunday, 20th July, 1947 at 2-30 p.m.

OFFICIALS :
A. C. U. Steward :
H. & D. M. C. Steward : J. Oliver
Clerk of the Course : W. H. Mellor
Hon. Secretary of the Meeting : S. Killingbeck
Hon. Treasurer of the Meeting : Harold R. Wilson
Timekeepers & Handicappers : H. Peacock & G. R. Todd
Judges : Ald. M. Bloom, Councillors J. L. Longhorn, S. Metcalfe
  T. V. Oldfield, W. M. Meredith, Messrs. F. Elliott, Senr
  P. T. Goldsworthy, E. O. Edwards and J. H. Dalkin
Starter : E. Herbert, Junr.
Number Steward : S. Ilderton
Machine Examiner : W. Bowron
Paddock Marshals : R. Nesbit, H. Sickling, G. T. Smith and
  Club Members
Course Marshals : E. G. Pipe, A. Ingleby, R. F. Luke, and Club
  Members
Lap Scorers : K. R. Cox and Miss K. Trewhitt
Travelling Marshal : T. M. Stonehouse
Programme Stewards : Mrs. V M Mellor and Lacy Members
Telephone Marshals : S. J. Morfitt and T. James
Ambulance : St. John's Ambulance Brigade, British Red Cross

Official Programme - Sixpence

G. Reg. Todd, Printer, Regent Buildings, Park Road, West Hartlepool.

Shepherds Hill, Swainby, Knockout Climb, mid-1930s. Main Norton dealer Alf Armstrong, left in Wellington boots, looks on at a fine start of two Norton riders. Number 13 is riding an O.H.C. International model and No. 12 machine is an ES2, or Model 18. The Cleveland Hills and a good crowd make a perfect setting for this sporting day out.
Courtesy of Jack Wright

Frontispiece of the official programme for Middlesbrough & District Motor Club's event, Shepherd's Hill, Swainby, 1936.

SPEED HILL CLIMB AND CIRCUIT RA
on SHEPHERD'S HILL, SWAINBY,
for Solo Motor Cycles, Three Wheelers and Cars

BANK HOLIDAY MONDAY, AUG. 3rd,
at 2 p.m.

Yorkshire Centre Restricted Permit No. R 1385.
R.A.C. Invitation Permit No. 1651.

Official Programme ... Price TWOPEN

All events under General Competition Rules of the R.A.C (Four-Wheeled Cars) and A.C.U.

LIST OF COMPETITORS.

No.	Name.	Town.	Machine.
1	F. Randerson	Doncaster	O.K. Supreme
2	H. W. Redding	Norton/Tees.	Ariel
3	H. S. Cox	Leeds	Ariel
4	T. E. Oates	Leeds	O.K. Supreme
5	J. P. Sharp	Leeds	P. & M. Special
6	A. Bell	Middlesbrough	B.S.A.
7	H. Masheder	York	Francis Barnett
8	K. D. Hopkinson	Leeds	Triumph
9	W. Walker	Skipton	A.J.S.
10	F. W. Collyer	Stockton	Norton
11	E. G. Pipe	Middlesbrough	Ariel
12	C. G. Wheatley	York	Excelsior
13	R. Munro	Leeds	Velocette
14	G. Walton	Middlesbrough	Velocette
15	M. Cunningham	Middlesbrough	Velocette
16	Jack Brett	Leeds	Velocette
17	S. Flintoff	Bradford	Sunbeam
18	A. Edwards	Dewsbury	Norton
19	M. Randerson	Doncaster	Triumph
25	R. G. Abbott	Leeds	Stevens
26	J. Reynolds	Leeds	Stevens
20	W. Trotter	Castle Eden	Rudge
21	A. C. Lynn	Redcar	Norton or Douglas
22	H. Dancaster	Leeds	Rudge
23	W. Lye	Leeds	Douglas
24	J. Milns	Doncaster	Matchless
25	R. G. Abbott	Leeds	Rudge
26	J. Reynolds	Leeds	Rudge
27	J. E. Russell	Thornaby	Rudge
28	E. Massheder	Pateley Bridge	Rudge
30	R. S.Steavenson	Middleton S. Geo.	Steavenson Special
31	Harry Souter	Sunderland	Frazer Nash

68

Reg Harkness in an MG on a timed hill climb at the Shepherds Hill incline event, 1930s.
Courtesy of Robin Cook

Robin Steavenson at the wheel of his "Special", Swainby Incline, 1937.
Courtesy of Robin Cook

John Steavenson in "Special 2", Swainby Incline, Whitsuntide 1938.
Courtesy of Robin Cook

FRED RIST: THE ALL-ROUNDER

Fred's father was the proprietor of the old established motor garage business of Fred Burr in Middlesbrough. Sales included motor car, motorcycle and cycle sales and the firm was agents for Beeston Humber, Sunbeam, Rover and Napier cars and later Coventry Eagle and Sunbeam motorcycles. Fred had his first ride on a two-stroke Royal Enfield motorcycle, which he rode around the poultry farm where his family lived near Stokesley, North Yorkshire. He quickly built up his confidence which stood him in good stance in years to come.

On leaving school in the late 1920s and early 30s of the Depression years Fred started his apprenticeship as engineer at the local Dorman Long steel works at Cleveland. He joined the Army and was posted to the Royal Tank Corps at Bovington where he met Lawrence of Arabia. When travelling home on leave he used a 350 cc Humber on loan from his father's garage, and later a 493 cc B.S.A. Sloper, to cover the round trip of 700 miles to Teesside. Fred started his trials riding career whilst at Farnborough in 1938 and as a member of the Army team taking part in that year's I.S.D.T., winning a gold medal. He was again selected to ride in the 1939 army team staged in Germany in the closing weeks before the outbreak of war. He and other B.S.A. team members were instructed via the British Embassy to break off from the competition and make for the Swiss border as soon as possible. They finally made it back to England with only days to spare before war was declared on 3rd September.

In the early post-war years Fred became manager for Pallister, Yare & Cobb motorcycle sales on Linthorpe Road, Middlesbrough. They were agents for B.S.A., Enfield, D.O.T. and many others. He was a popular rider at local events and it wasn't long before he left and moved to Birmingham, continuing to ride for B.S.A. in many types of event, including trials, scrambles, and grass track. He even took part at an early Olivers Mount meeting at Scarborough, winning the handicap. In summer time he loved to compete at any sand race meeting being staged at that time. Always B.S.A. mounted, he made a profound impression on the national sand racing scene, riding his B.S.A. B32, B 34 and 650 A.10 Specials. His string of successes is well-documented in the history books. He retired from his own motorcycle business which he had opened in Neath, South Wales. Born and bred on Teesside Fred was, without doubt, one of the top British riders of his era who made an indelible mark on British Motor Cycle Sport.

Fred Rist on his 250cc B.S.A. at a scramble in the Cotswolds, 1949.
Courtesy of Bob Light

73

THE REDCAR AND DISTRICT MOTOR CLUB

Little is known of the origins of the club before World War Two, except that a club did exist in the town. Its secretary was a Mr. Curtain, who lived in Widgeon Street, Warrenby. The Club met in the Red Lion Hotel in the town. Motoring activity mainly consisted of road trials and social runs. The post-war Redcar Club was reformed in the early Fifties. It was affiliated to the East Yorkshire Centre of the A.C.U. and its membership grew from a handful of keen motor enthusiasts to probably 50 members. The club leased a plot of land on the railway excursion platform in Kirkleatham Street and purchased a large wooden ex-RAF building which they erected on the site. It was even fitted out with toilets and a small bar. Social events consisted of quizzes, dances in the Coatham Hotel and tramp's suppers.

A full programme of road navigation and night trials, as well as semi-sporting competitions, was organised. As the club grew more ambitious plans unfolded, which included: trials and scrambles at Slapwath, near Charltons; grass track events on the old firing range at Guisborough; and sand racing on Coatham Sands, Redcar. Gymkhanas were a novelty event on the rugby field, Redcar Racecourse and the field at the bottom of Redcar Lane, now known as the Ings Estate. It is uncertain why the club folded in the 1960s. Probably it had outgrown itself and members were expecting too much of the willing Committee, who couldn't devote the time for business commitments.

Jack Threadgall and girlfriend on their 350cc Matchless, taking part in one of Redcar & District Motor Club's Navigation Trials. This checkpoint looks like Pickering or Kirby Moorside High Street, North Yorkshire. Club officials appear to be asking the car driver some questions.
Courtesy of the Threadgall Family

By the late 1950s Jack Threadgall had changed his mount to a Norton ES2. Here he is taking part in a Club semi-sporting trial.
Courtesy of the Threadgall Family

Guisborough 'three-in-one' course makes local history

REDCAR MOTOR CLUB have made local history in the sport with their "three-in-one" project at Slapewath, near Guisborough.

The club has now obtained permission to use a fine stretch of farmer's land, on which they have a scramble course, grass track and a trials course. Something quite unique to Tees-side and the North Riding.

The scramble course has already had its "baptism" although when the second meeting ever to be staged there is held on Sunday, September 6, it will have something of a new look. A bulldozer has made a notable difference. Now it is much longer, wider and, as a result, faster, with the adverse camber removed, and an old quarry included. The course has, in fact, been extended by about 150 yards.

The new grass track "home" is in a field nearby, one which holds out big prospects to the club. The staging of the first racing there, however, is at present held up owing to a full programme of events by the other clubs in the East Yorkshire Centre of the A.C.U., and to avoid any clash the inaugural meeting is likely to be delayed until the end of next month.

And, finally, to course No. 3—for sporting motor-cycle trials. This, when established, should be a fine headquarters for the rough riding enthusiasts, and with moorland, mud and water in good supply, there is plenty of scope for many first-class trials in the future.

Officials in the Redcar club have said a sincere "thank you" to Farmer Herbert Jackson, brother of club captain Bob, for an acquisition which might prove a spur to the other clubs in the area, to follow suit.

Newspaper article about Redcar Motor Club's events at Slapewath, near Guisborough.
Courtesy of the Evening Gazette

An excellent view of a meeting in progress, watched by a good crowd, at Redcar Motor Club's scramble course at Slapewath. The dry dusty conditions kicked up by the racing added to the spectacle. Note the rider leaping the brow of the hill, with daylight showing under his wheels!

Arthur Williams, motorcycle dealer in Gresham Road, Middlesbrough, was a good all-rounder but was a particularly determined scrambles rider. He competed on a number of different makes of machine including D.O.T., Matchless, D.M.W., and his own 2- stroke Special (A.W.S.). He notched up a considerable number of firsts in the 1950s and early 1960s before he migrated to Australia in 1964.
Courtesy of Arthur Williams.

Peter Dent from Carlton-in-Cleveland, on his James, leads the lightweight field down Hangman's Drop under extreme dusty conditions at the 1955 Slapewath Scramble.

Peter Hodgson, on a 350cc Gold Star B.S.A., leads around Hollybush Corner, 1955.

An ex-US Air Force Dodge Crew Bus makes an excellent grandstand for Redcar club members at the Sand Races, about 1953. Seated on the roof are (left to right): Albert Lynn; Derek Thomson; unknown; Peter Charlton; Colin Horsfall; David Keane (rider) leaning on the door; Maureen Marshall in a white duffle coat; Ann Marshall; Ken Marshall with glasses; unknown in white pullover; the author in overalls; Eddie Ransome on left with goggles; and Ian Denny in white overalls

Members of Redcar Motor Club attending the Gymkhana on Redcar Racecourse, July 1956. They are (left to right): Derrick Smith; Barry Andrews; Ron Southeran (?); Bob Kendrew, Howcroft Walton; John Coverdale; Brian Sempler; David Jowles; Keith Bradley; and Joan Thirwall.
Courtesy of Evening Gazette.

Whitby Regatta early 1950s. All part of the fun of this annual event which took place on the small patch of sands to the north of the harbour. The local motorcycle shop of Watkinson's organised this gymkhana, which was open to anyone who cared to come along and have a go. The gymkhana was always held on the Monday of Whitby Regatta week. Participants are (left to right): Jack Threadgall (Matchless); Reg Raw (B.S.A.); unknown; George Raw (James); Henry Lyth (James); starter unknown; and unknown (A.J.S.).

Courtesy of the Jack Threadgall Family.

STOCKTON AND DISTRICT MOTOR CLUB

The club was founded in 1930 and with a close proximity of Middlesbrough it is hardly surprising that a large portion proportion of its members were also Middlesbrough club members. The records that I had at my disposal fell short of my expectations regarding information on the club's pre-war activities. However, some of the club's surviving records from 1946 to the 1950s are of interest.

The first post-war club AGM was held at Percy's Café, Thornaby. Later meeting nights were held in the YMCA for a short period and finally club rooms were rented in King Street, Thornaby, until 1956. The pattern of club life fell into a regular weekly social occasion, with a good variety for all i.e. inter-club quizzes, darts, dominoes, beetle-drives, as well as talks and film shows. The sporting drivers were equally well catered for, with a mixed bag of road navigation and night-trials, usually run once a month. The first post-war speed event was a grass track meeting held on Easter Monday 1946. No venue is given, but it is thought to have been at Billingham Bottoms, just off the A19.

The club's first major national event was in November 1946, when, in conjunction with the Middlesbrough and District Motor Club, they played a considerable roll in the organisation of the first post-war Scott Trial at Swainby in Cleveland. Their combined involvement in the Scott continued annually until 1950, whence it was transferred into the capable hands of the Darlington Motor Club. The Stockton Club staged a scramble at Bishopton, Stockton, in 1947. In 1951 it appears that the club had a run of misfortunes in finding a permanent plot of land to stage off-road events, but, as luck would have it, the Hartlepool Motor Club came to the rescue with an offer of Greatham Airfield to stage a grass track meeting. Approaches were also made to the Redcar and District Motor Club for the use of their scramble course at Slapeworth, near Guisborough. Also, the Thirsk Club helped with the offer of use of their Sandy Lane Farm grass track course.

The trials scene was somewhat better, as land in Billsdale, Gribdale, and around Castleton frequently used by the Middlesbrough and District Motor Club, was offered for use to the Stockton Club. The Lion Inn on Blakey Ridge was an ideal start and finishing point. The annual Boxing Day Fancy-dress Trial in Billsdale was always tremendous fun.

The Club's calendar also shows that the gymkhana events were quite frequent in the summer months, support being given to the Northallerton clubs event for the War Memorial Fund. Other venues for gymkhanas were Guisborough Cricket Field and a spot near Rosedale. Events for 1953 showed it to be a busy year, with 10 sporting trials for motor cycles and four main road trials for cars/bikes. In later years emphasis was focused on road safety rallies and production car sporting trials. It is recorded that excellent grass track racing meetings took place at Seamer near Stokesley, Cleveland.

All the excitement and party atmosphere can be felt at the Gymkhana in this apple-bobbing race, with water flying all over. It's uncertain at which Club event of the mid- to late-1920s this photo was taken.

This is probably Stockton Motor Club's first dinner dance at the Maison De Dance Hall 1930. The J.M. on the wall over the stage shows that it was the Jack Marwood Band playing. Machines were new models from a local dealer (left to right): Arial; Royal Enfield; Velocette, with Horace Reading seated; next Norton; and a New Henley, with Jimmy Graham.
Courtesy of Wallace Holmes

Photographs are few and far between of Stockton Club events! A number of grass track race meetings did take place at Seamer, Stokesley. This action shot shows No.111, Roy Cunliffe and passenger, Peter Wilson, on a Norton or Ariel/J.A.P., about to overtake Dave Owen riding a Norton/J.A.P., May 1959.

Courtesy of Sheila Cunliffe

THE SCOTT TRIAL

The Scott Trial, traditionally staged in West Yorkshire since 1914 and running through to 1937, gained the reputation of being the toughest one day trial in the world. Due to various circumstances, one of which was the expansion of suburbia in the Dales, the trial made a move to the Cleveland Hills, promoted by the Stockton and Middlesbrough Clubs. The two Clubs worked well together, many of the members being in fact members of both Clubs. Jack Gash was the Clerk of the Course and, with an army of willing helpers, prepared a course over two laps of a 20 mile circuit of a demanding course, starting at Swainby, which lived up to the Scott Trial tradition of the old West Yorkshire event. The winner of this 1938 Scott was Len Heath Ariel, who completed the course in 3hrs 38mins. Best performance by a Middlesbrough Club Member was Fred Rist, winning the Gazette Trophy. The 1939 trial was cancelled due to the start of the Second World War and not until November 1946 was the Trial resumed on the same course as 1938.

The winner for 1946, 1947 and 1949 was Irishman Bill Nicholson, on a B.S.A. The 1948 Trial was won by P.H.Alves for Triumph. Regrettably the Trial was discontinued in Cleveland after 1949 and transferred to the Darlington and District Motor Club who took responsibility for organising the event with the start at Richmond, running over a 65mile course, attracting two hundred entries. The Scott was firmly established in Swaledale and Arkengarthdale, and the Club successfully ran it for forty years until 1990 when it was handed over to the present organisers, the Richmond and District Motor Club.

MAP OF COURSE (2 Circuits)

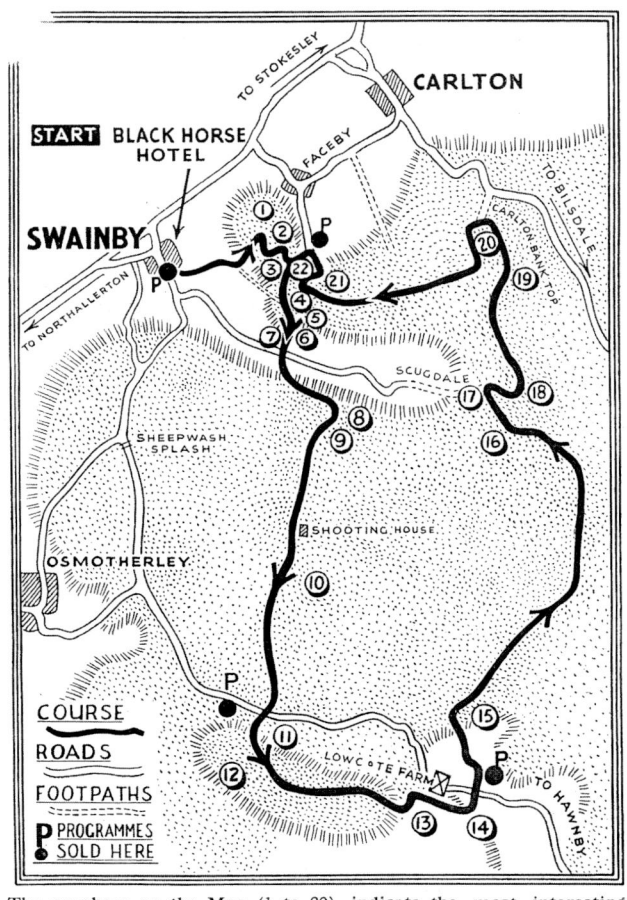

Map of the course of the Scott Trial, 1946.

The Scott 1938. L to R Bill Ryan, Len Heath (The Winner), Williams, Jefferies, Little, Rawlen
Courtesy of Middlesbrough & District Motor Club

Jack and Connie Gash with family at Sheepwash near Swainby, Cleveland, in 1935. This was a popular picnic site for Teessiders. Over this area the local clubs staged their winter season trials. Jack was a tireless worker and organiser for the Middlesbrough club as captain for many years.

Geoff Duke in a relaxed manner ploughs through the rocky stream whilst taking part in an early Scott Trial. It is interesting for Norton fans to note that the engine in the 500T frame is the big 4 side valve model which Geoff says was a bit of an experiment. He hoped to get more 'plonk' which would help but because of the extra weight the idea was abandoned. Geoff Duke spent much of his early motorcycle days in and around Teesside whilst serving his army service at Catterick. He became a member of the Middlesbrough Motor Club, riding in several club trials and events, and trying his hand at Cleveland Park speedway track. He later went on to work at Norton's in Birmingham, riding with Rex Young in many national trials before Geoff became fully engaged in a Works road racing team and later becoming world champion.
Courtesy of the Wilf Barker Collection

Stanley Woods from Ireland riding a 197cc James Commando. Stanley was world famous for his achievements in road racing and equally successful in other sectors of motor sport, including trials. He was a regular visitor to the Scott and always returned home with some silverware.
Courtesy of the Wilf Barker Collection/Bill Hutton

The photographer picked a perfect spot to capture Rex Young, on his 500cc BSA, wading through a section of a late 1940s Scott Trial in Scugdale.
Courtesy of the Wilf Barker Collection/Bill Hutton

The scene is set for what is thought to be the Middlesbrough & District Motor Club's first Cleveland Trial in 1952. Riders lined up outside the Royal Oak in the High Street, Great Ayton, are (left to right): No. 24 Colin Dunne (Francis Barnet) joking with John Bean; Gordon McLauglan, smiling; No. 12 Alec Clacher; No. 1 Alan Walker (Norton); No. 2 Rowlands (A.J.S.); No. 6 Harry Chilvers (James); No. 8 Ron Pipe (Norton). Note the lady at the upstairs window observing the excited crowd.
Courtesy of the Evening Gazette

International stars Rex Young, a work's Norton rider from Middlesbrough, with Johnny Brittain, a Works Royal Enfield rider, surrounded by schoolboy autograph hunters at the start of the Cleveland Trial in the High Street, Great Ayton, 1952.
Courtesy of the Evening Gazette

THE DARLINGTON AND DISTRICT MOTOR CLUB.

The Darlington and Bishop Auckland Motor Club arrived on the north eastern scene in 1905. Evidence of the Club is a pre-World War One report of a large Club contingent attending the annual 'Richmond Meet', an event where northern enthusiasts congregated to share an interest in the hobby. The Club, like many others, lapsed during World War One and afterwards reformed as The Darlington Motor Club. The Club's modem-day links with Croft go back to 1927, when they staged their first grass track racing event just behind the Working Men's Club in Croft Village. Later, other meetings were staged at Willow Bridge, Barton, adjacent to the A1. The economic depression of the period was affecting the number of entries in all types of motor sport, which necessitated the cancellation of some of the Club's planned activities.

At the same time, a South-end Motor Club existed in the same town. It also suffered through the economic depression and had financial problems in the 1930's. It was decided to amalgamate with the main Darlington club, the outcome being a much stronger body which was able to arrange a mixed bag of car and bike events, as well as the usual round of social and other events, such as film shows, beetle drives, and whist drives.

Once again, the Club lapsed with the Second World War and in 1946 it was reformed under the chairmanship of John Neasham. The early post-war years, with petrol rationing in operation, were difficult times and, to help stimulate club interest, the first events were trials using pedal cycles, which were all good fun. But the Club was planning bigger things and, by 1950, had secured permission to organise motor racing at Croft Airport, as it was known then. The first event on 6th May 1950 was for sports racing cars and was a great success. This was followed, on Saturday 19th May, by the first motor cycle race meeting, which attracted some 125 entries, and 3000 spectators. It was described in the motoring press as "Yorkshire's Silverstone". Events continued successfully until 1958 when the M.O.D. closed it for motor sport. Not deterred, the Darlington Club successfully acquired nearby Catterick Camp and also staged race meetings at the Thornaby Airfield, which consisted of separate events for cars and motorcycles.

MAP OF COURSE

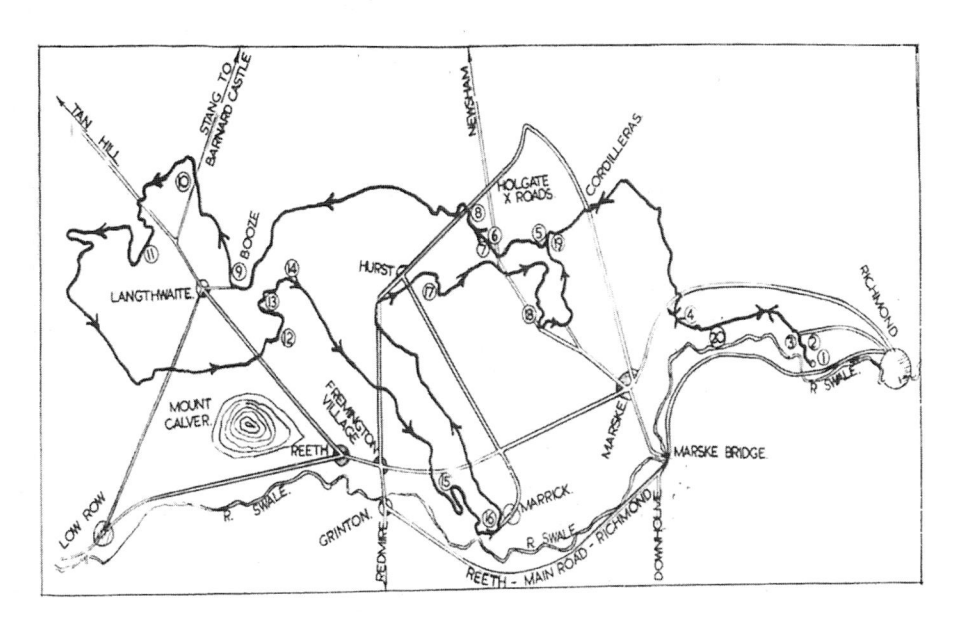

Map of Darlington Club's first Scott Trial, 1950.

Works rider Bob Ray, on a 500cc Ariel, wades through the River Swale in full flood, probably Darlington Club's first Scott Trial in 1950.
Courtesy of the Wilf Barker Collection/Bill Hutton

The remote Swaledale Moorland is the setting for this photograph of L.E. Jarman, tackling the Hell-Holes section on his 197cc James, 1956.
Courtesy of Alf Kirby

Croft Airport Circuit in 1950. The first events at Croft Airport in 1950 for both cars and bikes were staged on a track laid with straw bales on corners and by 1963 under new management a more permanent circuit was established until recent years when it was modified again to the one we know today.
Courtesy of Jack Wright

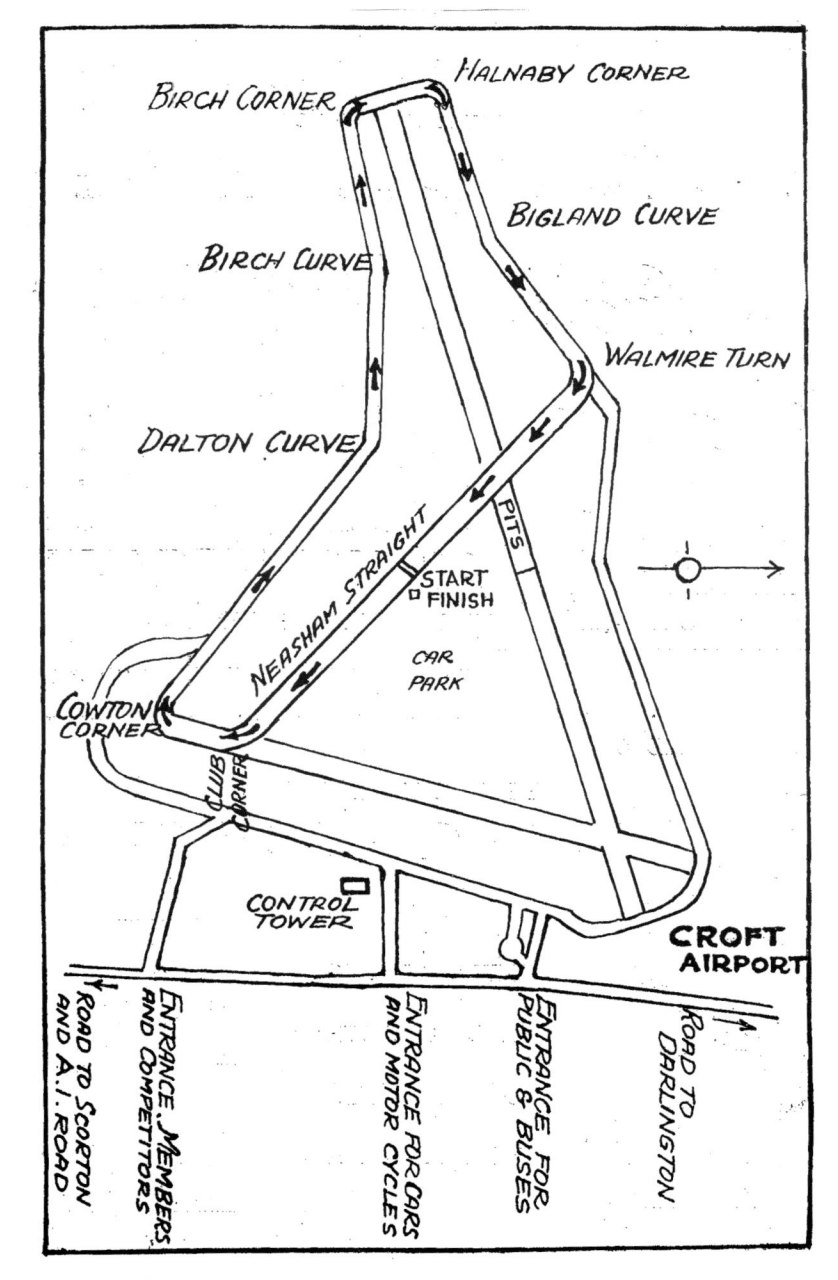

Croft Circuit in later years. The current layout is different again.

The First Darlington & District Motor Club Croft Sports Car Meeting, 1950. E.J. Newton returns to the paddock in his 1971cc Frazer-Nash B.M.W. Le-Mans replica after winning his class for cars up to 2,000cc with a speed of 65.58mph.
Courtesy of Jack Wright

Line up for the Y.S.C.C. Meeting Sports Car Unlimited event at Croft in 1951. Second in line is Peter Collins who broke the course record with his Cadillac-Allard at 74.64mph.
Courtesy of Jack Wright

Racing on a wet miserable, bleak airfield are not the ideal conditions, but this delightful 328cc B.M.W. made it worthwhile for Blackpool Solicitor, Norman Buckley, with a 3rd place in the race for Sports Cars up to 2000cc at Croft in 1950.
Courtesy of Jack Wright

E.I. Appleyard chats to friends before his event at Croft in which he achieved second place in the Sports Car Unlimited race. This Jaguar XK 120 is the actual car that won the 1950 Alpine Rally.
Courtesy of Jack Wright

Alan Rodgers coming into the pits after winning at the 1950 Croft meeting, steering his 500cc Cooper with one hand and holding on to the fuel pipe at the same time.
Courtesy of Jack Wright

Alan Rogers, winner of the race for 500cc racing cars at the Y.S.C. Meeting in 1950, works at the back end of his J.A.P.-engined Cooper's tail cowling after having dragged it behind him in the previous race for five laps. It is said that it sounded like a skeleton dancing on a corrugated iron roof!
Courtesy of Jack Wright

CAR TRIALS

The Darlington Club was quite active with their car reliability trial events on Gandale Moor. A small band of locals made up the entry of enthusiasts who mainly competed in home built specials made from Ford 10 powered cars, Austins and Jeeps as well as Jowett Javelins. Some bought the first production Delow trials specials, also trials cars made by Buckler, Canon and King Craft. The Roderick Gray Trophy was the premier award of the Darlington car trials scene.

The ubiquitous 747cc Austin Special was quite a popular choice for the D.I.Y clubman to enter into the four-wheel branch of motor sport at an affordable level. This example was owned by E.A. Bragge and raced at Hartlepool Sprint in 1950.
Courtesy of Jack Wright

The Darlington Club's Roderick Gray Trophy Trial on Gandale Moor, Catterick, March 1954. Bert Cryer, winner of the event, tackles two tricky sections in his Ford Special
Courtesy of Wilf Barker Collection.

HARTLEPOOL & DISTRICT MOTOR CLUB

It is almost impossible to give an exact date when the club was founded, however, it is certain that it was at the start of the 20th century. From the existing records that have survived the ravages of time, the yellowing pages show a prolific amount of historical information on all aspects of the Club's activities from 1939 to 1951, which is within living memory for some readers. For the non-competitive club member many joint car or bike road navigation and night trials were staged, along with regular social events throughout the year. For the more motor sport minded, there was the choice of motorcycle grass track racing at Greatham Aerodrome and also at Elwick Showfield and Crimdon Park.

With the ending of World War Two, West Hartlepool Corporation requested the Club to stage a grass track on Greyfields Rugby Field to coincide with the victory celebrations in the town on June 8th 1946. Unfortunately the weather was far from perfect, with light rain for most of the day, and racing was postponed for one hour. However, after requests from the Mayor of Hartlepool, the Club officials decided to run the event, after first laying sand on the slippery course, even though it was still raining slightly. The racing was the best the Club had ever staged. It was considered that the track was far better than the field at Elwick. The Ghyll in Elwick village was used for motorcycle scrambles and, later in the day, a separate event and sections for cars. In conjunction with the town's carnival week, the Club staged motor cycle and car sprints on the lower promenade, which was very popular for many years, attracting several leading names from the racing world.

Marshals assist rider No.9 whilst Peter Lloyd, with an injured ankle, recovers himself from the mud. Both machines are A.J.S. Photographed at the Ghyll in Elwick.
Courtesy of Peter Lloyd

Rex Young gets his Garden Gate Manx Norton airborne at the Elwick scramble track in 1948.

Ginger Fowler, a Middlesbrough clubman, gets down to it on his 1939 Triumph Twin. Ginger would ride this bike every weekday and use it on weekends for all types of competition, even hitching a sidecar to the bike for a spot of grass track racing. In this Hartlepool event he had a loan of a Works-tuned engine.
Courtesy of Ernie Fowler

In the early post-war years sprint meetings were few and far between. The annual Hartlepool event attracted drivers from far and wide. These photographs, taken by Redcar amateur photographer Jack Wright, have captured the atmosphere of the era. The relaxed attitudes on safety are noticeable, with no straw bailing and little crowd control needed, all adding to an enjoyable event. The Hartlepool Sprint Tourist Class event, 2nd August 1947 with (left to right): 1st J.A.M. Clark on a 998cc Vincent; 2nd Bill Zealand on a 346cc Triumph.
Courtesy of Bill Zealand

Denis Parkinson from Wakefield, riding No.4, an Excelsior Manxman, competing against Edwards, on a Norton, at the first Hartlepool Promenade Sprint in 1938.
Courtesy of Mortons Motor Cycle Media

A cold windy overcast sky didn't deter these riders enjoying themselves on the wet Seaton Carew sands in the 1950s. Middlesbrough clubman No.16, Don Harker, keeps pace with Sammy Wilderspin, Hartlepool clubman in this 350cc race.
Courtesy of Don Harker

This giant of a race car was driven by Tony Brook of international car racing fame. The two pushers seem to have brought the Vauxhall Villiers Supercharged monster into life to get to the start line in time for its first practice run, 1950.
Courtesy of Jack Wright

C. Tipper in his delightful little 498cc Mondeo single overhead camshaft Norton Special.
Courtesy of Jack Wright

Rear view of the Mondeo Norton Special. Note the individual chain drives to the rear wheels through the Norton gearbox.
Courtesy of Jack Wright

97

A fine action shot of Jim Lafone in his 1934 Q Type supercharged 750 M.G. at the Hartlepool Sprint. Only eight of the Q-Type Midgets were made, producing almost 150 B.H.P. and capable of something like 138 mph. Jim Lafone hailed from Kendal and was a regular competitor in the northern speed events in the Q Type M.G.
Courtesy of The Automobile

Mr. Warburton, representing the Scottish Sports Club in his big V8 Allard, had a successful day out at Hartlepool in 1949. Note No.43, a 500cc H.R.D. Cadwell Special leaning against the wall which is probably George Brown's machine.

J. Arnold, in a Bugatti, set a new record at 14.08 seconds over a 660 yards course on 2nd August 1947. His getaway, accompanied with terrific wheelspin, had to be seen to be believed and was all the more remarkable when it is remembered that he started in third gear!

SPEEDWAY RACING ON TEESSIDE

The speedway boom that came to England from Australia in 1928 rapidly spread throughout the country. On 23rd August of that year the promoters, Albion Auto Racers, staged the first meeting at the Cleveland Park Stadium, Middlesbrough. This was something completely new to Teesside and the local press made big of the fact that the famous riders from Australia Sig Schlam, and Ron Johnson, would be the star attractions, along with several northern pros.

In all 33 riders took part in this first ever 'Dirtrack' event, as it was known, in Middlesbrough. The outcome was that it became a huge success, which the public loved. The bark of the open exhausts, coupled with the smell of the methanol fuel and Castrol oil, all added to the heady cocktail and thrill of the spectacle of four riders fighting for the lead. When the starter's flag dropped they jockeyed for the lead into the first corner of a four lap race, sending a wave of cinders flying over the crowd on the corners, whilst broadsiding their machines in the leg-trailing style that was very spectacular, adding to the terrific excitement of the crowd.

Many of the local riders taking part later became big names in the Speedway World, once the league system was set up in 1929. Riders from Middlesbrough and surrounding areas were: the Creasor brothers, Freddy and Walter, both riding A.J.S. machines; Harry Whitfield (Sunbeam) an exponent of the foot-forward style of cornering; Albert Smith (New Henley); Frank Thompson (A.J.S.); Bill Collinson (New Henley); J.R. Smith (Ariel); and Phil Blake (A.J.S.). The two names absent on the night of the opening meeting were Jack Ormston, from West Cornforth, and Norman Evans, of Kirby-in-Cleveland, known as the most well-dressed man in Speedway. These two, with Jack Ormston, Norman Evans, and Harry Whitfield, were to become synonymous with Speedway Racing on the World stage in years to come. All of them, at one time or another, represented England in the Test Matches, both at home and abroad. At the same time, this new sport of Dirtrack Racing was welcomed by most locals, particularly as the season started when the football season was almost over, and filled the summer Thursday night entertainment gap.

VOTE FOR
JOHNNIE BROUGHTON
FRANK CHARLES
LARRY COFFEY
BROADSIDE BURTON
BUSTER BREAKS
CHARLIE BARRETT
ALEC HILL
FRANK HARRISON
NORMAN EVANS

Sure Candidates for the
CLEVELAND PARK
(Speedway Division).
FRIDAY NIGHT next
May 31st, at 7-30 p.m.

Labour Exponents of British Skill and Pluck.
Liberal Cinder Shifters.
Conservative Trophy Holders.

Admission (including Tax): Popular Enclosure 1/-.
Both Grand Stands - 2/- each.
Ladies and Children half-price to all parts.

Poster seen on bill-boards around Teesside publicising Middlesbrough Speedway in 1929, probably coinciding with an election year.

Two pioneer speedway riders from Middlesbrough over in Sydney, Australia, demonstrate the art of sliding the corners at the Royal Showground track in 1930. On the inside is a little-known, Middlesbrough's Cliff Parkinson and well known Harry Whitfield on the outside. Both represented England in the Test matches
Courtesy of Daily Telegraph AEP Publishing PTY Ltd.

However, it was a pity that the sport came at the same time as the world industrial and economic depression, which hit Teesside very hard with mass unemployment, and Speedway seemed to decline, with dwindling attendances. But, to get some idea of Speedway's popularity, the bigger London clubs seemed to weather the Depression period well, still attracting large crowds. Jack Ormston, Harry Whitfield and Norman Evans, moved with the Times and all secured good jobs with a London clubs, quickly becoming extremely successful and earning huge amounts of money. In 1935 for example, Jack Ormiston, signed a contract for the Hall Green Birmingham Team, for £2,000 plus £100 appearance money, and was given a first class train ticket by sleeper from Kings Cross to Darlington after each match. The promoters were also to supply two machines plus a mechanic, who was Middlesbrough's Ronnie Parkinson, noted for his outstanding mechanical abilities with the preparation of racing engines, while in the real world miners were going down the pit for 25 shillings a week, and a labourer was working for £1 a week. But still fans managed to scrape together the bus fare, plus one shilling entrance fee and enough to buy a programme, and perhaps have a penny left over for a bag of chips on the way home.

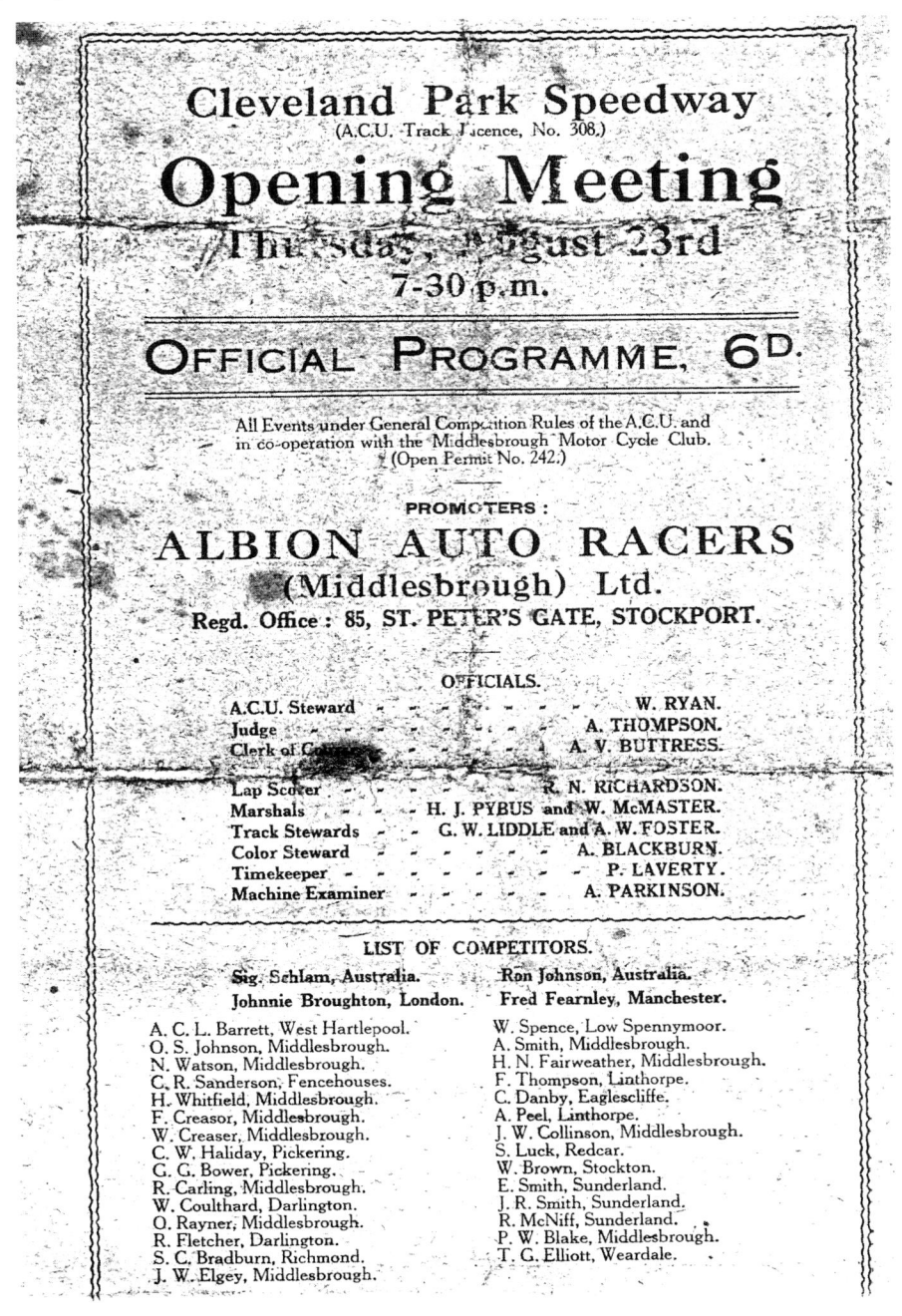

Cleveland Park Speedway
(A.C.U. Track Licence, No. 308.)

Opening Meeting
Thursday, August 23rd
7-30 p.m.

OFFICIAL PROGRAMME, 6D.

All Events under General Competition Rules of the A.C.U. and in co-operation with the Middlesbrough Motor Cycle Club.
(Open Permit No. 242.)

PROMOTERS:

ALBION AUTO RACERS
(Middlesbrough) Ltd.
Regd. Office: 85, ST. PETER'S GATE, STOCKPORT.

OFFICIALS.

A.C.U. Steward	W. RYAN.
Judge	A. THOMPSON.
Clerk of Course	A. V. BUTTRESS.
Lap Scorer	R. N. RICHARDSON.
Marshals	H. J. PYBUS and W. McMASTER.
Track Stewards	G. W. LIDDLE and A. W. FOSTER.
Color Steward	A. BLACKBURN.
Timekeeper	P. LAVERTY.
Machine Examiner	A. PARKINSON.

LIST OF COMPETITORS.

Sig. Schlam, Australia.   Ron Johnson, Australia.
Johnnie Broughton, London.   Fred Fearnley, Manchester.

A. C. L. Barrett, West Hartlepool.
O. S. Johnson, Middlesbrough.
N. Watson, Middlesbrough.
C. R. Sanderson, Fencehouses.
H. Whitfield, Middlesbrough.
F. Creasor, Middlesbrough.
W. Creaser, Middlesbrough.
C. W. Haliday, Pickering.
G. G. Bower, Pickering.
R. Carling, Middlesbrough.
W. Coulthard, Darlington.
O. Rayner, Middlesbrough.
R. Fletcher, Darlington.
S. C. Bradburn, Richmond.
J. W. Elgey, Middlesbrough.

W. Spence, Low Spennymoor.
A. Smith, Middlesbrough.
H. N. Fairweather, Middlesbrough.
F. Thompson, Linthorpe.
C. Danby, Eaglescliffe.
A. Peel, Linthorpe.
J. W. Collinson, Middlesbrough.
S. Luck, Redcar.
W. Brown, Stockton.
E. Smith, Sunderland.
J. R. Smith, Sunderland.
R. McNiff, Sunderland.
P. W. Blake, Middlesbrough.
T. G. Elliott, Weardale.

Official Programme of the Opening Meeting at Cleveland Park Speedway, 23rd August 1928.

In the mid-1930s, Jack Ormston, together with Tom Bradley Pratt, opened Middlesbrough Speedway again, and several open meetings took place in the following years. The promoters, eager to attract the public to these special events, advertised interval attractions to entertain the crowds. Some extremely amusing and apparently downright dangerous stunts were staged but apparently were great crowd-pleasers. An American stunt team, led by Put Mossman, known as the Crazy Gang, assisted by Peewee Cullam the clown, performed various stunts. Putt Mossman, clad in white leathers, raced his four-cylinder in-line Henderson down from the grandstand roof on a wooden ramp into a tank of fire in the centre of the track with less than 15 inches of water in it. This sensational stunt was followed by other tricks by members of the team who would ride through flaming hoops of fire, among other things. Mossman then proceeded to climb up and down a ladder fixed onto the rear of his Henderson, with the machine in full control circling the track. Many famous stars from the film, radio and sporting world were also another means of attracting the public and added glamour and thrill to speedway racing, the evening culminating in a grand firework display. Many of the second division tracks booked this type of interval entertainment, which doubled the attendances and saved some Northern tracks from extinction.

Portrait of Harry Whitfield taken in later years when he was manager of Middlesbrough Speedway.

Signed photograph of Cliff Parkinson.

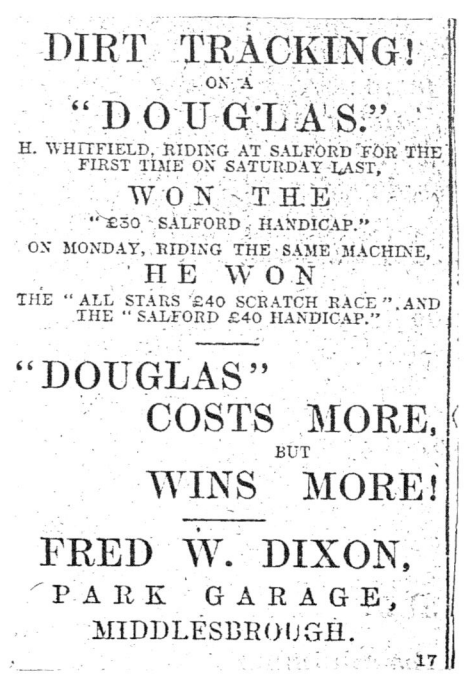

Newspaper cutting "Dirt Tracking! On a Douglas".

Jack Ormston from West Cornforth in his heyday. He was not a stylist rider but still won races with ease.
Courtesy of Bob Light.

Team Line up for Newcastle Speedway in 1929, which depended largely on riders from Teesside. Left to Right Fred Creasor, Phil Blake, Walter Creasor, Ernie Smith, Tommy Storey, Percy Dunn. The Creasor brothers also owned a butchers business in Newport Road, Middlesbrough.
Courtesy of the Newcastle Chronicle and Journal Ltd.

Norman Evans with his wife Flo, probably at Brough Park, Newcastle, where Norman was team captain for many years. The couple lived in Kirby-in-Cleveland and off the track Norman was known as the dandiest star of speedway. In post-war years Norman's machines were maintained by Joe Mace of North Ormesby.
Courtesy of the Evening Gazette

Norman Evans posing on an unusual machine, a 500cc V.Twin James made specially for speedway, in his early days at Cleveland Park, Middlesbrough.
Courtesy of John Sumervill/Colin Greenwell

105

Jimmy Kirby with the Fred Dixon tradesmans box outfit on which he serviced all the northern speedway tracks in the 1930s with Douglas speedway spares. Note the spare wheel and tyres on the back. This photograph was taken on Low Lane, Acklam, Middlesbrough, by Jimmy's brother Alf.
Courtesy of Alf Kirby

Eva Asquith of Bedale posing with her friend Ann Whitfield. Eva was without doubt one of the most outstanding women speedway riders ever. She travelled the world and won a whole host of cups and medals against some of the best male riders. Eva rose to fame in 1929, winning races in Denmark, South Africa and Spain, riding speedway Douglas machines.
Courtesy of Bedale Museum

Advertisement for Putt Mossman, "America's Greatest 'Stunt' Rider", 28th August 1936.
Courtesy of Middlesbrough Reference Library

With hostilities over after the Second World War, speedway racing came back to Cleveland Park with a bang. The sporting world starved for entertainment. Fans, new and old, flocked back in unbelievable numbers to see speedway racing again. Sometimes gates in excess of 10,000 were common. Harry Whitfield, now a retired rider, donned the mantle of promoter/manager. Happily quite a high proportion of riders from pre-war years were eager to get back into some serious racing again.

The Middlesbrough team, better known as the 'Boro Bears' of 1946, were: Left to Right 'Kid' Curtiss, Eddie Pye, Phil Dargue, Len Tupping, Wilf Plant, 'Tip' Mills, Geoff Godwin, Frank Hodgson (Captain), Jack Hodgson (Brother), Jack Gordon, with team reserves at back, Peter Lloyd, Fred Fewsdale - all of who made up an extremely successful team of racers. This was borne out by them winning the Northern League Championship for 1946 and 1947 and finishing third in 1948.
Courtesy of the Evening Gazette

Three generations of the Hodgson family (left to right): Frank, Jack, Laurie, and the little boy on the bike is Russell, who later became a Boro' team rider.
Courtesy of Peter Hodgson

DIRT TRACK OUTFITS

"JAGROSE" ACE MASKS
BEST TAN LEATHER
FREE BREATHING
SPLINTER PROOF
SIGHTS **10/6**

"JAGROSE SAVUS" CRASH
HELMETS. STAMPED
AND PASSED BY A.C.U.
42/-
ALSO CHEAPER QUALITY
STAMPED A.C.U.
21/- AND **27/6**

WELL PADDED SHOULDERS
AND ELBOWS

CLOSE FITTING NECK

DETACHABLE
WELL PADDED, EXTRA
ELBOW PADS **5/-** PAIR

LANCER PATTERN FRONT
FLEECY LINED

WELL PADDED SIDE
TO BREECHES

WELL PADDED KNEES

BLACK HORSE HIDE
SPECIAL DIRT TRACK
GAUNTLETS **7/6** PAIR
SUPERIOR QUALITY
10/6 PAIR

BEST TOUGHIDE,
3 STRAP TOP BOOTS
EXTRA STRONG
27/6

DETACHABLE
EXTRA KNEECAPS
WELL PADDED
5/- PAIR

STEEL TOECAPS,
DOUBLE WELDED,
WELL FITTING
5/6 EACH

DIRT TRACK SUITS

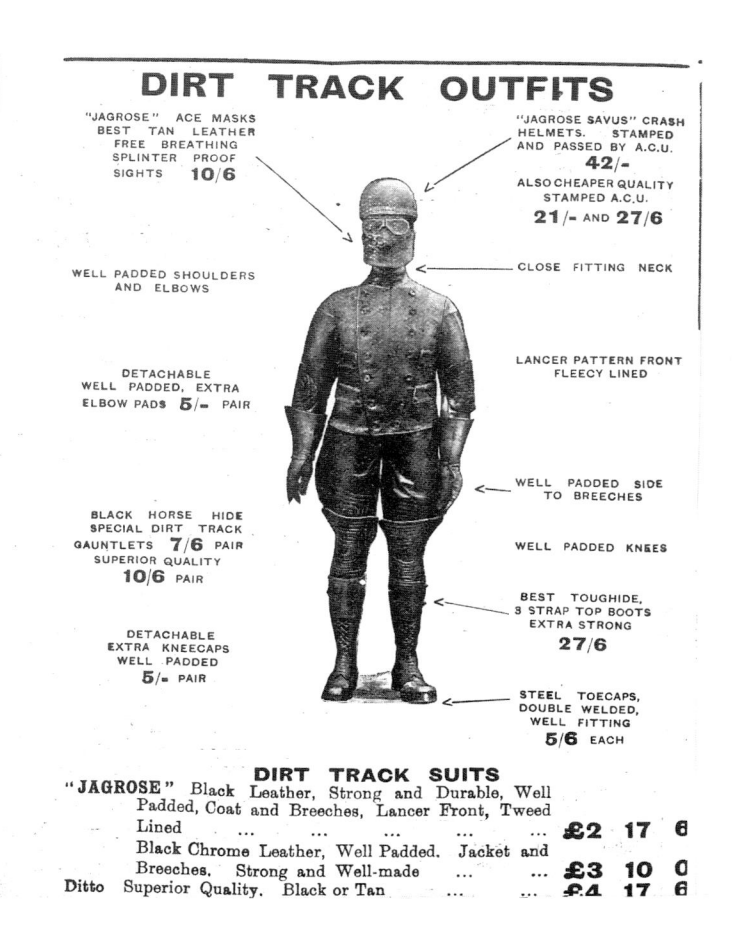

"JAGROSE" Black Leather, Strong and Durable, Well Padded, Coat and Breeches, Lancer Front, Tweed Lined **£2 17 6**

Black Chrome Leather, Well Padded. Jacket and Breeches. Strong and Well-made **£3 10 0**

Ditto Superior Quality. Black or Tan **£4 17 6**

What the well-dressed dirt track rider wore in 1930. This advert was included in the Upton's Motorcycle Shop catalogue of 1930 to cater for the boom in dirt track racing in the north east.

THE
MIDDLESBROUGH AND DISTRICT MOTOR CLUB
present
THE SEVENTH DIRT TRACK
MOTOR CYCLE RACE MEETING
under the General Competition Rules of the A.C.U. Permit No. E.Y. 440.

GUILDHALL POLICE DOGS

AT CLEVELAND PARK STADIUM
MIDDLESBROUGH

THURSDAY, 26th JULY, 1956, at 7-30 p.m.

PROGRAMME ... SIXPENCE

Programme for "The Seventh Dirt Track Motor Cycle Race Meeting", 1956.

The interval attraction at Cleveland Park by the Royal Signals Display Team from nearby Catterick was always spectacular. The popularity of speedway has always had its ups and downs over the years. The Middlesbrough Motor Club did organise meetings at Cleveland Park on a number of occasions, with a variety of riders and also some entertaining interval attractions, including spectacular firework displays as a finale to the night.
Courtesy of the Evening Gazette

Three local riders, with No.5, Peter Lloyd out in front, fight it out for the lead on the first corner.
Courtesy of Peter Lloyd

The Boro Bears locked in battle with the Edinburgh Monarchs in a league match watched by a large crowd at Cleveland Park, August 1960. Wayne Briggs leads the Boro pair, Tommy Roper and Bob Webb, into the first bend.
Courtesy of the Evening Gazette

Programme for a 1952 Middlesbrough v. Newcastle Midget car racing meeting, or Flying Bombs as the public called them. This sport became popular in this country in the post-World War Two years. Teams were set up throughout the country and staged on the same speedway tracks as the town's normal meetings, that is Middlesbrough's Cleveland Park and Brough Park, Newcastle. These machines were very spectacular and thrilling to watch and looked to have a great future, with proposals to set up a league. However, this was not to be and the new sport gradually lost favour in the North.

SMITH'S MOTORS, NEWCASTLE

J. S. Smith
presents

MIDGET and SIDE CAR RACING
at
CLEVELAND PARK

Middlesbrough v. Newcastle

7 P.M.

Thursday, 17th April, 1952

Official Souvenir Programme — 6d.

111

Midget cars in action somewhere in the north of England. These cars must not be confused with the popular 500cc Cooper type road racing cars of the period, as they had no similarity in design or construction. The cars were officially known as Skirrow 'Specials', having four wheel drive and powered by a 996cc Twin J.A.P. engine.

Popular Jack Faulkner in his ex-Dixon Riley 9 prior to his 1948 Redcar Speed Trials debut, where he gained a second place in the one mile sprint.
Courtesy of John Faulkner.

A group surround cars and their drivers at Coatham Sands, Redcar, in 1947 (left to right): Alan Ensol, standing next to a J4 type M.G. Midget, but not the car he raced; unknown man in white overalls; Wilf Hewitson, Monteleray Midget M.G.; and Bill Wilson S S Jaguar
Courtesy of John Faulkner.

Crowds gather on the finishing line to see R. Robinson in an M.G. Special at speed, Coatham Beach, Redcar, 6th July 1946.
Courtesy of Ted Walker (Ferret Fotographics)

A good action shot of Jack Faulkner in his Riley 9 leading M.G. driver No. 4 Approaching the bottom corner of Coatham Beach.
Courtesy of John Faulkner.

Oscar B. Moore in his O.B.M. Spcial which was fitted with a 328cc B.M.W. engine, leads Jack Faulkner, Riley 9. These Photographs were taken about 1950, probably on Coatham Beach, Redar.
Courtesy of John Faulkner.

The Robinson Sykes entry from Leeds, a 1286cc M.G., being off-loaded at Coatham Beach, Redcar, 6th July 1946.
Courtesy of Ted Walker (Ferret Fotographics)

THORNABY AERODROME

When the end of car sand racing came in 1955 the Middlesbrough & District Motor Club were left with a huge gap in their speed event calendar. It wasn't until the M.O.D. released nearby R.A.F. Thornaby, for use for motor racing in 1959 that the Club staged its first road race meeting, swapping the whine of jets for the roar of exhausts. The Evening Gazette reporter Bernard Gent, who wrote a weekly motor sport column, reported that 160 competitors had entered for this August 9th meeting, having the biggest entry for any event run by the Club before. It was an extensive mixed programme for motorcycles and cars round the airfield course. Thornaby road racing continued for three years until nearby housing development forced the Thornaby Council to withdraw permission for the Club to stage any further meetings.

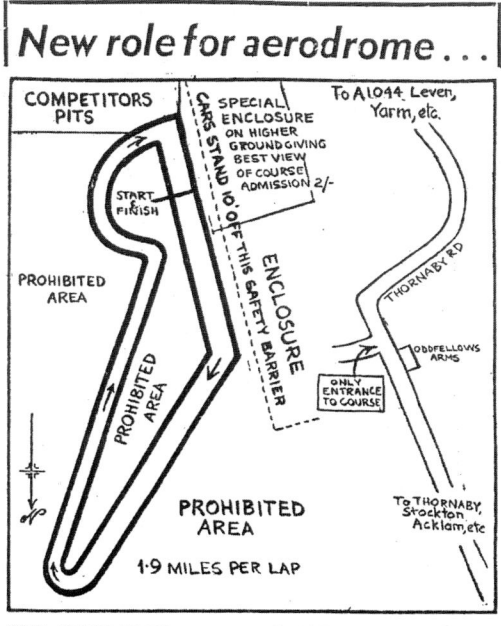

A mixed bag of riders in the paddock holding area, Thornaby. Amongst all the British hardware, the lone German-made 250cc N.S.U. 37 looks impressive.
Courtesy of Kevin Bentley

Plan of Thornaby Aerodrome course, 1959.
Courtesy of the Evening Gazette

116

The first batch of 250cc riders waiting in the assembly area to go out for the first race, Thornaby. The mechanic of Ariel Arrow rider, No.12, warms the bike up while the rider sits composed. Rider No.44, on his Ducati, is probably watching his rev. counter.
Courtesy of Kevin Bentley

Frank Harrison's F.H.N. Special, an inexpensive project made up of the following: G.N. chassis; 19" wheels on a Morris Eight front axle; a 1172cc modified Ford Ten engine with an ex. R.A.F. cabin blower for a supercharger but no gearbox; and a G.N. chain drive, giving four forward speeds which were fairly even and well suited to the power unit. He ran the Special on methanol, which it drank through an S.U. carburetta. Engine lubrication was castor oil based. Total cost was less than £150. The Special was used extensively around Teesside with a fair amount of success, namely at Croft, Catterick, Hartlepool, Redcar and St. Andrews.
Courtesy of Ian Denney

Frank Harrison astride his Douglas. Before Frank became known for his successful F.H.N. Special he had also been a celebrated pioneer speedway rider at Cleveland Park, Middlesbrough, in 1929, and as a member of the International Touring Team at various tracks on the Continent. In fact, he later adopted the track name of "Yank" Harrison as it sounded as though he was an American Team Rider. Early post-war motor sport enthusiasts remember Frank for his garage at Tunstall in Richmondshire and his racing car special.
Courtesy of John Sumervill/Colin Greenwell

Two outstanding names come to mind from Teesside car racing scene in the 1950's and 60's, both of whom were Garage owners. Jimmy Blumer above, traded from Roseberry Service Station, Acklam Road, Middlesbrough and raced a number of different make cars at local events, notably: Austin Healey 100's; 3442cc Lister Jaguar; 933cc Ford Rochdale; and 1960cc Cooper Monaco with Coventry Climax engine, at Thornaby, Croft and Catterick circuits. Here he is sat in a 1960cc Cooper Monaco, 1960.
Courtesy of Jimmy Blumer

After driving the D-Type Jaguar to the meeting at Croft, Alan Ensoll removes the windscreen before racing. Alan Ensoll, from Low Grange Garage, South Bank, raced several cars, including the Mk2 MG, the famous Gammon TC MG, Monza Lister and several Jaguars, XK120, C and D Types. Alan also built two Ford 10 Specials, one for trials and the other for speed events
Courtesy of Alan Ensoll

An Austin Healey in close pursuit of a Jaguar XK120 at Croft in the mid-1950s.
Courtesy of Alan Ensoll

What has this photograph got in common with motorsport? Scissor Grinder, Tommy West, toured the streets of Middlesbrough in the 1920s and 30s, pursuing his trade. Note the Billboards advertising Battle Axe tobacco and the Empire Theatre Summer Show. Also on the left is a large speedway racing poster for a World Championship Speedway, June 1930s.